sports cars

sports cars

on road and track
Ray Hutton

Hamlyn

London New York Sydney Toronto

Contents

Published by the Hamlyn Publishing Group Limited
London · New York · Sydney · Toronto
Astronaut House, Feltham, Middlesex, England
Copyright © The Hamlyn Publishing Group Limited, 1973

ISBN 0 600 38039 4

Printed in Great Britain by
Sir Joseph Causton and Sons Limited

Easier Done than Said . . .

Books like this usually start by attempting to describe what is meant by the term 'sports car'. The definition has defeated many learned students of the automotive art, and in times when the situation was more clear cut than it is today. By picking this book up you declare that you have some notion of what a sports car is; most people have. There are no rules set out here for what can and cannot be included under this very loose heading. Examples have been purposely drawn from a very broad field—one which has been referred to, even more vaguely, as 'high performance cars'.

But 'high performance' can cover a multitude of characteristics. If for example speed is a criterion, there are many heavy limousines which can travel faster and accelerate more rapidly than a low-priced open two-seater. They are not included here. Those that are range from super-powerful racing cars, through expensive, exotic Grand Tourers to cheap, stark build-it-yourself specials and 'souped up' versions of quite mundane production saloons. They all have perhaps just one characteristic in common—for whatever reasons, they provide, or have provided, a minority with something

more pleasurable to drive, more satisfying to control on a road or a track, than the basic transport used by the motoring majority.

Speed *is* an important factor, whether it be out-and-out straight line speed or the car's ability to reach point B from point A quickly. So is the type and style of the body—the sometimes misleading outward manifestations of whatever performance the car can produce. And as that wise commentator of the motoring scene Ronald Barker once pointed out, if there is ever any doubt whether a vehicle is a sports car or not, an insurance company will soon give a judgement. It is an unfortunate fact of life that the statistics employed by those hard-faced gentlemen single out for special treatment and often absurdly high premiums the very cars discussed here—cars enjoyed by enthusiasts the world over. Cars which are generally well maintained by owners who care more about the skills of driving than the average motorist.

But even in dispensing with an exact definition of a sports car there are certain machines on the fringes of the subject which are not within this book: the strangely compelling world of the American hot rod;

buggies—both for romping around roads and beaches and as serious contestants in off-road races like the Baja 1000; the specials used for that peculiarly British activity, the sporting trial—the only form of motor sport which does not have speed as a factor; 'funny cars' and dragsters; and some of the more specialised forms of racing two-seaters.

That there is such a wide range of individualist cars available in this mass-produced age is commendable, but for the future the prospects are less bright. Man's first love affair with the motor car is over. The vast favourable effect it has had on human life is beginning to be taken for granted and recently an increasing body of opinion has called for greater controls on the car's use and suggested theoretically sensible, if unpalatable, alternatives to this most convenient means of private transport. At the same time, controls, created in the first instance by the US government, on car safety and air pollution are causing significant changes to the everyday car and, for economic as well as technical reasons, are reducing the choice of models offered by the manufacturers. Sports cars, like any minority group, tend to suffer most.

In the Beginning

All cars in the early days of motoring were, in a sense, sports cars. They were not called that of course, but you had to be something of a sport to drive one at all. Despite protests of justification from their enthusiastic owners, in the dawn of motoring it was usually quicker and more reliable to take a horse-drawn buggy than one of the 'infernal com-

bustion' horseless carriages. Those early pioneers bought and enjoyed the imperfectly developed motor car not as a convenient means of transport but as a new mechanical hobby. It was natural that they should want to pit their machines against those of their neighbours. Thus motor sport was born.

A form of organised motor race

took place as early as 1894. Cars before the turn of the century were of very modest performance; 20mph was a daring speed. The first official Land Speed Record, set in France in 1898, was a stirring 39·24mph. In Britain, even after the 'Red Flag Act' had been repealed in 1896 there was an overall speed limit of 12mph. And while Continental Europe enthu-

siastically took up the idea of motor racing and hosted the great city-to-city races (which ended with the accident-scarred Paris–Madrid in 1903), racing as such has never been allowed on the public roads of the British mainland. It was in France, and to a lesser extent Belgium and Germany, where the sporting use of the rapidly maturing motor car took shape.

The first truly international race in the British Isles took place near Ballyshannon, Ireland in 1903 and in its winner we can see the beginnings of the sports car as it later came to be known. The occasion was the fourth in the series of Gordon Bennett races, which had started in 1900

Opposite: The first real sports car? The Mercedes 'Sixty' was a two-seater carrying the minimum of bodywork and no weather protection. A car of this type won the important Gordon Bennett Trophy race in 1903

Below: Very modern in appearance and performance for its day—the 1912 'Alfonso XIII' Hispano-Suiza. It had a four-cylinder engine of 3·6 litres and a maximum speed of 72mph

as a national team competition for a trophy presented by the American newspaper publisher James Gordon Bennett. In 1902 the Gordon Bennett was run from Paris to Innsbruck in Austria as part of the longer Paris–Vienna race and had provided a surprise win for the British Napier driven by S. F. Edge. Under the rules of the competition Britain had to play host to the race in 1903, and a special Act of Parliament had to be passed to allow the Irish roads to be used. The winning car was a Mercedes.

For the development of the first Mercedes we have to thank a wealthy Austrian businessman called Emil Jellinek who lived, in some style, in Nice. Among his many business interests was the sale of Daimler cars to his affluent Riviera neighbours. It was at his instigation that Daimler produced in 1901 a car with many important innovations, such as a steel channel chassis (in an age of wood construction), a proper 'gated'

four-speed gearbox, more than usually efficient brakes and a honeycomb radiator. He guaranteed enough sales to make Daimler's production of such a car a viable proposition and in return called upon them to name it after his young daughter–Mercedes. This first 35hp model was superseded by the famous 'Sixty', which incorporated further refinements and used a 60hp engine. This was a car of very real performance, as Alfred Harmsworth, later to become the newspaper proprietor Lord Northcliffe, demonstrated by recording a speed of 74·3mph at the Nice speed trials in 1903. It was one of these 60hp Mercedes that won the 1903 Gordon Bennett.

The modern American adage that 'there is no substitute for cubic inches' had been responsible for the steep rise in the speeds of cars in the first years of the 1900s; engine capacities simply became larger and larger in cars intended for racing and by 1906 there were several examples

The 'Red Devil' Jenatzy before the 1903 Gordon Bennett Trophy in Ireland at the wheel of the borrowed Mercedes in which he won the race

in the 18-litre range. The 1903 Mercedes Sixty, with its 9·2 litre four-cylinder engine, was quite modest in comparison to these, but it offered one of the largest engines generally available in a production car. It had sufficient flexibility to be used for leisurely touring as well as out-and-out racing, thus meeting one of the criteria on which sports cars have traditionally been judged. However, the demands of competition were soon to create a more powerful 90hp version of the car, with a 12·2 litre engine, and it was this model that the factory had intended to enter in the 1903 Gordon Bennett race. But in June of that year the Daimler works at Cannstatt was almost completely destroyed by fire and with it went the works racers. Clarence Gray Dinsmore, an American who was one of the distinguished list of Mercedes owners, loaned his Sixty to Daimler for their top driver Camille Jenatzy to use in the race. It bore the very minimum of body-work—the engine cover, two seats and a fuel tank—but, by all accounts, had a pretty standard chassis and engine. It beat the giant racing cars of the day and specifically the 13·7 litre Panhard of the Frenchman René de Knyff to win at an average of 49mph.

Events fit for royalty

By 1905 Britain had the Tourist Trophy, held in the Isle of Man on a circuit which had been used for the eliminating trials to choose the Gordon Bennett team the previous year. The TT was an event intended for touring cars and for the first few years set a limit on fuel consumption. Among the winners were names that one would not today associate with

motor sport: Rolls-Royce, Berliet, Rover. But more important to the development of the sports car were some sporting events which took place in Germany during the same period. An artist called Professor Hubert Herkomer had initiated a series of trials combining the elements of what we know today as rallying with timed speed tests and hill-climbs. These events were intended to encourage high performance four seater touring cars but then, as now, some thinly disguised racing cars appeared, and the handicapping was severely criticized.

The Herkomer Trials were continued in similar form as the Prince

Unfamiliar racer—the Hon. C. S. Rolls in the 20hp Rolls-Royce which took first place in a race at the Empire City Track, Yonerks, USA. Rolls-Royce produced models which could claim to be sports cars in those early days and won the Austrian Alpine Trial in 1913

Henry Tours from 1908 to 1911 with a trophy presented by Prince Henry of Prussia, a car enthusiast who had competed in two of the earlier events. The Prince Henry Tours were to give rise to a number of machines which are widely regarded as the first 'real' sports cars. But the rules still required them to be four seaters. In 1907 there was a race in Germany for *two* seaters complying with a set of rules which, because they set generous body dimensions, managed to eliminate out-and-out racing cars. This was the *Kaiserpreis*, donated by the German Emperor himself, who had looked approvingly at the results and interest created by the Herkomer Trials. Engine capacity was limited to 8 litres for the *Kaiserpreis*, which attracted over 90 entries, many specially built for this once-only event. It was won by the Italian Felice Nazzaro—one of the all-time 'greats' of motor racing—driving a car from the *Fabbrica Italiana Automobili Torino*. That company's cars were known as Fiats, as of course they still are.

The *Kaiserpreis* in 1907 encouraged the development of two seater sports cars. It was won by Felice Nazzaro driving a F.I.A.T. (later just Fiat) of 8 litres capacity. Removal of wings was allowed

It was the first Prince Henry Tour in 1908 which made clear the developing trend for sporting cars. Designers were turning away from the idea that rear seat passengers should sit higher than those at the front and they developed low, longer-wheel-base cars which accommodated all their passengers between the axles. Bulky, heavy items like running boards and wings were reduced to a minimum, producing cars that looked for all the world as if they were disguised racing cars. They were in a way—but they led to a style of car which was to be sold and recognised as 'sports' for nearly 30 years.

The Prince Henry Tours were remarkable events, rather leisurely in pace, with social as well as motoring purposes, since the route called at several stately homes. But they did become very important in prestige and publicity. A young man named Ferdinand Porsche had been appointed Chief Engineer of the Austro-Daimler company which was owned by the German Daimler firm. They had sold the cars of the parent company in the early years but with the arrival of Porsche the Austrian subsidiary became more self-sufficient. Porsche's first project was to produce a car for the *Kaiserpreis*. He modified a Mercedes chassis, and fitted a form of electrically actuated transmission.

This was not a success, but Austro-Daimler were keen to persevere and gave Porsche a clean sheet of paper to design a 'Prince Henry' car. This appeared in 1910, and was officially designated the 27/80. It had a four-cylinder engine of 5·7 litres with an overhead camshaft. It produced nearly 100 horse-power (which represented considerable efficiency for that time) and the 27/80 could exceed 80mph. Most important, it won the Prince Henry Tour, with Porsche himself driving and two other Austro-Daimlers in second and third places.

Less successful on that occasion but in many ways more significant in the long term was an entry of the British Vauxhall firm into the 1910 Prince Henry Tour. They too had a dynamic and talented designer – Laurence Pomeroy. In 1908 they entered a 20hp car in the RAC's tough 2 000 mile trial and in the following two years that car's 3-litre

This Hispano-Suiza was driven by Paul Zuccarelli to, win the 1910 French *Coupe de l'Auto* for *Voiturettes*. It was the direct predecessor of the 'Alfonso XIII' production car (see page 7)

Ferdinand Porsche was both the designer and the driver of the Austro-Daimler that won the 1910 Prince Henry Tour in Germany

four-cylinder side-valve engine was improved to give 60mph at 2 800 rpm (a very high engine speed in days when engine lubrication systems in particular were not well developed). The 'Prince Henry' C-type was a very different looking car from the 20hp, with a very low, skimpy and doorless open four seater body and a distinctive 'V' radiator. Compared to the Austro-Daimler it was down on power, having a smaller and less sophisticated engine; the Vauxhall could do about 65mph. It was shaft-driven while the first examples of the Austro-Daimler Prince Henry model used the time-honoured method of transmissions by chains and sprockets – like a bicycle. Vauxhall exhibited the C-type at the 1911 London Motor Show and it was the only British production car of its type on display – the term 'sports car' had still not come into general use. In 1912 the engine was enlarged to 4 litres and a year later to the order

of one Joseph Higginson, who wished to settle a private score by beating his rivals at the Shelsley Walsh hillclimb, Vauxhall built a 4½ litre version with an aluminium body and any frills which remained in the Prince Henry's sporting specification removed. Higginson got his record and Vauxhall took a similar car to the Brooklands track (which had opened in 1907) and were surprised to find that it could lap the banked circuit at 108 mph. During the following season this prototype developed from the Prince Henry did remarkably well in racing. A new production model was born and it was to be called the 30/98 (nobody is entirely sure to what the two figures refer). Very few were built

before the demands of the First World War put an end to private car production. In 1919 the 30/98 became a catalogued production car at a relatively high price of £1 475. Nevertheless it was to become a very successful model, which remained available until the 1925–6 general slump forced Vauxhall to make strict economies.

Though the various Prince Henry cars are the more obvious milestones of this era, there were other makers producing cars which fitted the sports car bill: Fiat and Isotta-Fraschini from Italy; the lightweight Hispano-Suiza 'Alfonso XIII', designed by a Swiss and built to delight a King in Spain; Métallurgique, Minerva, and Pipe from Belgium,

A big American – the 1908 Chadwick Great Six. It had an 11-litre six cylinder engine and some models were fitted with an early form of supercharging. The body follows the typical two-seater 'runabout' style popular in the USA

The Prince Henry Vauxhall was the first of a series of fine sporting cars from the British company. It led to the famous 30/98 which remained in production until 1926. The fluted bonnet top is a distinguishing feature

a country that today has no car manufacturers; Benz, who made available a chassis with a 22-litre engine of the type that had given them the Land Speed Record in 1912; Sunbeam's 12/16s, which had given rise to the cars which won the *Coupe de l'Auto* race in France.

In Britain Rolls-Royce had produced something that looked every inch a sports car, a version of the famous Silver Ghost which was used for a London to Edinburgh run achieved entirely in top gear. It was not a very powerful car considering its $7\frac{1}{2}$ litre six-cylinder engine, but it did do 79mph at Brooklands immediately after its Scottish journey and one suspects brought the quiet smoothness for which Rolls-Royces are renowned to a world which expected its sporting cars to be noisy,

Right: The Stutz Bearcat epitomised the sports car of America in the pre-1920s era. Both four and six cylinder engines were available, the 'four' being of $5\frac{1}{2}$ litres. Rivalry between Stutz and Mercer was intense

Below: A Bugatti first appeared in the 1911 Grand Prix de France. Small, light and precision built, it was the forerunner of a *marque* that was to become world famous. After World War I this type 13, with its overhead camshaft engine enlarged, became the Type 22 and enjoyed considerable competition success. The distinctive horseshoe radiator that characterises later Bugattis had yet to appear

harsh and rattly. In 1913 a British Talbot achieved the distinction of becoming the first car to cover 100 miles in the hour at Brooklands. The car was a stripped 25hp with a $4\frac{1}{2}$ litre engine which had one of the highest power outputs for its size of any available at the time – 130bhp was claimed, produced at the then-staggering engine speed of 3500 rpm.

On the other side of the Atlantic the most celebrated sporting cars were those of Stutz and Mercer, who waged battles both on the dirt tracks across the North American continent and in the publicity that attended them. In their earliest forms both the Stutz Bearcat and the Mercer Raceabout had the look of stark simplicity reminiscent of the Mercedes Sixty – a chassis with an engine cover, lights, wings, a couple of seats and a fuel tank. There was no scuttle and the windscreen, if fitted, was usually restricted to a 'monocle' mounted on the steering column. In some ways these American cars were the more obvious forerunners of the two seaters that were to become so popular in Europe during the next decade than the Prince Henry four seater tourers.

Europe had a crop of two seaters in the light car category, which like their racing counterparts were called *voiturettes*, while the even lighter cyclecars briefly flourished. Though England had its small car advocates, the *voiturette* class particularly thrived in France.

France was still a leader in technical innovations too. Peugeot introduced the twin-overhead camshaft layout so widely used for sporting cars today, in their 1912 Grand Prix racing car, while in 1911 a tiny, beautifully built 1327cc car with the sophistication of an overhead camshaft engine had appeared in the Grand Prix of France. It was an early Bugatti – the epitome of precision engineering with a delicate touch, completely at opposites to the brute force displayed by the heavy brigade, which was to flourish in Britain in the 1920s.

Golden Era

Recovery from the First World War brought a new zest to motoring and in the Roaring Twenties the sports car played a part in the much publicised life-style of the well-heeled young men of the day and their flapper girl friends. Motor racing thrived—particularly at Brooklands, where anyone from the owner of the most exotic racing machine to the tuned Austin Seven driver could find an event to suit him.

The biggest sales were inevitably of the smaller, cheaper two-seaters which became available in large numbers—the Austin Sevens in their many special forms, and later the first MGs. But among the most prestigious and expensive sporting

Right: The Type 37 Bugatti was a 1½ litre four cylinder model introduced in 1927 and also available in supercharged form as the Type 37A

Below: The stylish Atlantique coupé version of the Type 57 Bugatti appeared in 1937. It was one of the forerunners of today's GT style

cars there existed a conflict in design. Britain, thanks mainly to Bentley, produced the giants, the substantial four-seaters with cut-down sporting bodies that followed on directly from the 'Prince Henry' style. The Continent, and more particularly France, looked to Bugatti as the prime example of the way to achieve similarly high-performing results—small, light in weight, not necessarily the fastest in maximum speed but with great importance placed upon, and efficiency achieved in, roadholding and handling. Between the black Bentley and the white Bugatti there were, of course, many shades of sports car grey: some good, some bad, many since

11

There was no lack of innovators in 1920s—Gabriel Voisin built this extraordinary but aerodynamically advanced 30hp 2·3 litre two seater in 1924

forgotten. The choice was bewilderingly large.

These were surely the Golden Days for the 'proper' sports car. The widespread popularity of the style and the mass production that went with it brought a certain self-defensive pride, perhaps a snobbishness, to those who owned and appreciated the more exclusive, more carefully-built examples which went before. As early as 1934 a group of these enthusiasts—rather like those in America today who maintain that because of government restrictions the motor car has already reached its acme—formed the Vintage Sports Car Club, an influential organisation which was to concern itself only with cars made after 1918 and before 1931 (those built earlier being recognised as 'Veteran'). The VSCC was later to accept that some cars of merit were made in subsequent years and introduced the term 'Post-Vintage Thoroughbred' to describe pre-Second World War cars which they felt were 'made in the Vintage tradition'. The Classic Car Club of America recognises a similar category for some cars of the 1930s.

The vintage sports car had a recognisable shape and style, a lightness of form compared to its more lumbering touring counterpart. It was an open car with its emphasis on performance shown by its relatively long bonnet, outside exhaust and tiny aero screens. The suspension was hard, to make the best of the solid, non-independent axles front and rear and the leaf springs and friction shock-absorbers which were almost universal. Chassis frames lacked rigidity and engines were mounted solidly to them. But in the early 1920s the sports car was far from mature. True self-starters and proper electrical systems were widespread, but brakes were certainly an undeveloped feature and few cars had them on the front wheels. The old chain and sprocket drive was not dead either, though it was on the way out for the majority of makes.

The fastest catalogued car in Britain was still the 30/98 Vauxhall, which in 1922 was to be uprated from 90 to 112bhp by the use of overhead valves operated by push-rods. The Vauxhall 'Prince Henry' and its contemporaries were much copied by other makers and designers. W. O. Bentley will have given them more than a passing glance before building his first prototype which was tested for the first time in 1919. He admitted to close scrutiny of both the 1912 Peugeot and the 1914 Grand Prix Mercedes in designing its engine—a 3 litre, four cylinder with sixteen valves actuated by an overhead camshaft.

'W.O.' did not set out to build a sports car. He wanted a touring car 'with long legs'; one which would be capable of covering long distances effortlessly and at high speeds. Twenty-four hours flat-out was not, however, what he had in mind, and when told that John Duff, a Bentley owner, intended to enter a 24-hour race at Le Mans in 1923, he is reported to have dismissed the whole thing as 'crazy', predicting that no-one would finish because 'cars aren't designed to stand that sort of strain'.

History shows that Bentley was very wrong in his gloomy predictions. Duff and Frank Clement

W. O. Bentley tests the first 3-litre Bentley in January 1920. The production version of this car went to the first Le Mans 24 Hour in 1923 and won the race a year later, despite 'W.O.'s' initial scepticism

finished fifth in that first Le Mans 24-hour Race, held on the narrow and incredibly rough track some two miles longer than the circuit used for the 24 hour race today. The 1923 race was won by a French Chenard et Walcker at an average speed of 57·2mph.

Le Mans soon gained a reputation as one of the toughest motoring events and really did contribute to the development of the production car and its equipment. It started as the idea of a group of enthusiasts in France's 'insurance town', which had previously played host to the French Grand Prix races. In its early years competing cars were required to be one of at least 30 of that model to be built and all but the smallest had to have four seats (in fact, not until late in the 1930s could the largest cars be pure two seaters). Naturally the period of night racing made the best possible lights a necessity and there is no doubt that the race did much to advance lighting and electrical systems. Weather equipment was also required in those early races—and it was tested by a compulsory period when each car had to be run with its hood erect.

The Duff and Clement exploratory visit in 1923 was well worth while. The following year they went back with a new 3 litre Bentley—now with four wheel brakes—and won. 1925 saw the first official Bentley team but it was not until two years later that the fabulous run of four successive victories started. That was 1927 and the year of the White House crash. Until the extensive revisions which took place in 1971, *Maison Blanche* (White House) was notorious as a deceptively fast blind left and right flick on the return to the pits area. It was here that following an accident to a little French car, all three works Bentleys crashed— two (one 3 litre and a new '4½') ended in a ditch, but the third managed to get back to the pits with extensive damage and a bent front

In the early Le Mans events competing cars had to run the first part of the race with hoods erect. This is the start of the 1927 race, won— after the famous White House crash—by Bentley no. 3 driven by S. C. H. Davis and Dr J. D. Benjafield. Frank Clement's Bentley leads here

Left: The substantial chassis frame of the Speed Six Bentley

13

MG selection. The 1954 TF—last of the
traditional MGs—had more sweeping lines, in
its cockpit as well as its overall shape, than
its predecessors. These included the 1934 K3
and the 1931 18/80 four-seater, behind the
TF in this photograph

The 1934 Riley MPH was outwardly similar to the Riley Imp, but had a six-cylinder engine, initially offered in 1458cc or 1633cc forms. Later a 50bhp 1726cc unit was available. The body style shows more than a passing resemblance to contemporary Alfa Romeos. The engine (left) gave rise to the ERA racing power unit. This beautifully restored MPH belongs to BMW chief Bob Lutz

axle. Thirty minutes of repairs put it back into the race and 'Old Number 7' as this car was known, driven by Dr J. Dudley Benjafield and S. C. H. (Sammy) Davis chased a French Ariès through the night and won the race when it expired with less than two of the 24 hours left.

Le Mans successes made Bentley's name and ensured that his cars were among the most coveted of their day. The four cylinder, overhead camshaft, 3 litre Le Mans cars were short-chassis Speed Models also known as 'red label' (referring to the colour of the 'B' emblem on their radiators). There was a six cylinder 6·5 litre engine available for bigger cars known as 'Big Six' and later on a sports version of it called the Speed Six (green label) which won Le Mans in 1929 and 1930. Later still came the 8 litre Bentley—intended as a fast touring car but used by some for competition in more modern times— before Bentley Motors Ltd collapsed in 1931 and subsequently became part of the Rolls-Royce Group.

One of the renowned 'Bentley Boys', the wealthy amateurs who formed the backbone of the racing team, was diamond millionaire Woolf Barnato and he had previously 'bailed out' the company when it got into financial trouble. Another Bentley Boy, and the most successful racing driver of the group, was Sir Henry Birkin. He was responsible for the most famous Bentley of them all—the one that 'W.O.' didn't

Above: The duel at Le Mans in 1930 between the Mercedes SSK of Rudolf Caracciola and Christian Werner and Birkin's 'blower' Bentley. Both retired, but a Speed Six Bentley went on to win the race, the last of five wins for the company in the 24 hour classic. Like the Mercedes, the Bentleys sometimes appeared in single seater races with the wings removed

Right: Brooklands battle. The 4½ litre Bentley of S. C. H. Davis and Sir Ronald Gunter fought it out with Guilio Ramponi's 1500cc Alfa Romeo in the 1929 'Double Twelve'

want to build. This was the 'Blower 4½', the supercharged version of the 4½ litre, four cylinder engine which had been produced by chopping two cylinders off the 'Big Six'. Easily identified by the massive supercharger blower between the 'dumb irons' below the radiator, the Blower Bentley had a guaranteed maximum speed of 125mph–mightily impressive for a big, four seater car that weighed at least two tons. Only 50 were made. But they never achieved really significant competition success. The model's best performance was at Le Mans in 1930 when Birkin engaged in a classic duel with the German ace Rudolf Caracciola in a 7 litre Mercedes-Benz SSK; an Anglo-German contest that was to be repeated in the same race 25 years later between Hawthorn's Jaguar and Fangio's Mercedes. Birkin's Bentley and the lone Mercedes SSK both burnt themselves out in their 1930 battle and retired.

Brute force from Germany
The Mercedes SSK was one of the few Continental sports cars to follow

Bentley's 'bulldog' philosophy. It too was a big, weighty car with an emphasis on strength and power. The SSK had grown out of a series of cars designed by Dr Porsche when he joined the new union of Mercedes and Benz from Austro-Daimler. The first was the K model which was widely regarded as very dangerous; the better S model which followed gained a good competition record. The 1928 SS, also known as the 38/250, was called the SSK in short-chassis sports car form (K

standing for *kurz* in this case). Its 7 litre six-cylinder engine was supercharged (a system of increasing power output which Mercedes had been the first to introduce on production cars in the early 1920s) and gave about 200bhp, which was roughly equivalent to the Speed Six Bentley. Like the Bentleys, these cars also appeared in Grand Prix-type races, for during the period these were sometimes run as *Formule Libre* events, meaning that anything went. Caracciola finished a surpris-

ing third with this big and unmanageable car in the first race round the tight little streets of Monaco in 1929. The final extension of the SS was the SSKL, a lightened and more powerful (300bhp) version, which unlike the previous models, was never made available for sale. The factory cars won sports and Grand Prix races and finally it was fitted with a high but streamlined single seater body for races on fast circuits in 1932. This special car achieved no less than 156mph at the

banked Avus track at Berlin. Two years later Mercedes were to change completely the face of racing with their ultra-scientific Grand Prix cars; the days of the racing 'juggernaut' were numbered.

But even if racing cars became highly sophisticated overnight, the big road sports car remained in the pre-Second World War catalogues. The 3 litre Sunbeam was not long gone and had been a significant design, although it never achieved the competition results of the

Competition in Britain. Tiddlers racing at Brooklands with a baby Austin Seven in the foreground and a Bugatti giving chase

Bentley, to which it was equivalent. Together with the French Ballot company, Sunbeam were the first firm to put a twin overhead camshaft engine into production, and their 3 litre engine also had twin carburettors and a dry-sump, meaning that it was fed oil from an outside tank under high pressure like today's racing engines. The firm of Invicta also sold big-engined sports cars, with a 4½ litre as their basic model; a car of good performance but not altogether impressive road stability. Like the cars of Lagonda, Invictas used Meadows engines. The most notable success for the Lagonda '4½' was a win at Le Mans in 1935.

Mercedes retained big sporting cars in their range but they became progressively bigger–or at any rate heavier–without making advances in any other directions. The 500 and 540K cars of the middle and late 1930s were fashionable fast transport for the German politicians but they were no longer real sports cars. On the other hand, there was a handful of manufacturers in France who at this time built big-engined sports cars of considerable merit. These included Delage, Delahaye, Hotchkiss and Talbot (known as a Darracq in England to avoid confusion with the British make of the same name) and they were spurred on by late 1930s resurgence in sports car racing which came when manufacturers realised that they could not compete with the Germans in Grand Prix racing.

Bugatti–an artist-engineer
But one can scarcely discuss French cars of the between-Wars period without reference to Bugatti, whose cars enjoyed a following and *mystique* perhaps greater than any other *marque* in motoring history.

Ettore Bugatti described Bentley's efforts as 'the fastest truck in the World'. The British Bulldog was the complete antipathy of the ideas of this Italian-born artist-engineer who worked from Molsheim, a village in the disputed territory of Alsace. When the Germans were

advancing on Molsheim in 1914 he had physically buried three of his latest 16-valve four cylinder Type 13s. After the War was over these cars embarked on a highly successful competition career and were easily the fastest light cars of the time. With its engine enlarged from 1·3 to nearly 1·5 litres, the Type 22 development of the Type 13 was capable of nearly 100mph. In 1921 these cars took the first four places in the Italian Grand Prix for *Voiturettes* at Brescia and the model subsequently became known as the 'Brescia'.

In England in the early 1920s a young man named Raymond Mays was making a great name for himself in hill-climb events with a pair of much-modified Brescia Bugattis. Mays went on to become one of Britain's most famous racing drivers, to found the ERA racing project and subsequently the BRM Grand Prix car. His Bugattis also preceded another modern trend. They were called *Cordon Rouge* and *Cordon Bleu* after the brands of champagne and brandy of those names. But unlike the highly-priced sponsorship of today's racing teams, Mays insists that the only payment he ever received was the occasional gift of a few bottles of the products!

The Brescia succeeded not only because of its high performance and light weight, but because it possessed precise steering and unusually good roadholding. On the debit side it had little in the way of brakes and was exceedingly uncomfortable and noisy. The 1923 Type 30 set another important Bugatti trend—the straight eight cylinder engine. This was used in the famous all-enveloping 'tank' racing cars which appeared in the French Grand Prix that year and were timed at 117mph—this with a 2 litre engine

The Type 30 gave rise to that

Contrasting Bugattis. *Top:* In hill-climbs Raymond Mays achieved considerable success with his two Brescia Bugattis, modified by Amherst Villiers and known as *Cordon Bleu* and *Cordon Rouge*. The picture shows Mays at Shelsley Walsh

Left: The streamlined Bugatti Type 57G which won the Le Mans 24 Hour race in 1937 and 1939 was directly related to the coupé shown on page 11. Jean-Pierre Wimille, who won both races, stands alongside

most successful and well-known of all Bugattis, the Type 35, which dominated European racing from 1925 to 1930. It used an improved straight eight 2 litre engine with three valves per cylinder and was developed through a long series of models including the 35B, a supercharged 2·3 litre version. The Type 35 was really a Grand Prix car, but in those days conversion into a road-going sports car required little more than fitting a set of cycle-type wings, so that such cars are legitimately road sports cars. The proper production sports car version (usually with four seater Grand Sport body) was called the Type 43. It was one of the first genuine 100mph cars to be sold to the public and had vivid acceleration to match.

In the early 1930s Bugatti adopted the twin overhead camshaft layout for the Type 51 and this led to the Type 55 production counterpart with a 2·3 litre engine, 135bhp and a maximum speed approaching 120 mph. Usually fitted with an elegant swept-wing two seater body, the Type 55 is regarded by many followers of the *marque* as the most outstanding Bugatti sports car. The Type 57, introduced in 1934 was the last real production Bugatti; 750 examples were made in various forms, from touring saloons to 130 mph supercharged sports/racing,

and the Type 57G cars with their slab-sided aerodynamic bodies won Le Mans in 1937 and 1939, the latter at 86·8mph with a 3·3 litre 57C supercharged touring car engine.

By 1939 Bugatti's reluctance to move with the times was showing badly. Though as well constructed as ever, his cars never had independent suspension in the modern sense, they stuck to semi-elliptic leaf springs front and rear, the 57 had a slow and old fashioned gearbox, and Bugatti did not adopt hydraulic brakes (and thus gain braking that was really equivalent to his cars' performance) until 1938. Ettore Bugatti died in 1947 and subsequent attempts to produce a postwar version of the 57 never properly materialised.

The Alfa Romeo 8C2300 – the '2·3' – succeeded the firm's 1750 racing sports car. Here Taruffi trails dust in the 1932 Mille Miglia

It is worth observing that no Bugatti was ever made with left-hand drive, and that most of the more expensive Continental cars of the pre-Second World War period had right-hand drive, despite their countries' opposite rule of the road. It was not until 1956 that Lancia, who had started building their fine and rather unconventional sporting cars in the 1920s, finally made the change. Some competition-type

sports cars also retained the central accelerator which had been a feature of many makes in the 1920s and continued on Italian racing cars well into the 1950s – difficult if one regularly drove more than one make!

The smaller challenge

Bugatti's main challenger in sports car events of the late 1920s and early 1930s was Alfa Romeo. The Italian firm had the classic 1750, available with one or two camshafts, supercharged or unsupercharged, which won among many events including the Tourist Trophy and the Mille Miglia. It was succeeded by the '2·3', a twin-cam supercharged straight-eight which took on Bugatti's role as the most successful sports car, winning Le Mans four times from 1931–4.

After the Bentleys Britain had little to offer in the over 2-litre class, though the Georges Roesch Talbots made in London were good – conventional but carefully designed, and closely related to the equivalent saloons, Talbot 105s finished third three years running at Le Mans. Then there was the 1931 2½ litre Speed Twenty Alvis, successor to the popular 'duck's back' 12/50 and the Alvis front-wheel-drive racing cars. The SS Jaguar appeared in the mid-1930s as a fast, reasonably priced, quite refined but slightly flashy two-seater, while there were Anglo-American hybrids like the Railton and Brough Superior.

There were more British candidates among the 1½ litre cars. Aston Martin produced an expensive, conventional 1½ litre car which handled nicely and eventually grew to 2 litres, joining AC, whose six cylinder engine first appeared in 1919 (and was still available in the Ace in 1963!). Small six cylinder cars were fashionable and Wolseley, Singer and Riley were among those who offered them. Rileys made four and six cylinder sports cars ranging from 1100cc to 2 litres. The 'sixes' included the short-lived MPH model which shared its basic engine with Raymond Mays' 'White Riley' racing car – the forerunner of the ERA, Britain's most successful racing car in the years immediately before and after the Second World

War. The Frazer-Nash, which had grown out of the earlier GN cycle-car, was light and fast, with remarkable acceleration and the unorthodoxy of chain drive long after other makers had abandoned it. It too could be had with a six cylinder $1\frac{1}{2}$ litre engine (the Blackburne), but more usually Meadows four cylinder units were fitted. The most famous chain gang 'Nashes were those modelled on the car entered in the 1931 Ulster Tourist Trophy and known as TT Replicas. They have a large and loyal band of supporters today. H. R. Godfrey, one of the founders of GN, became involved with the HRG—a throw-back to the 1920s produced between 1936 and 1956.

The Tourist Trophies in Northern Ireland, which started in 1928, were important to the development of the small British sports car. A Lea-Francis won the first of this series, Riley won for two years in 1935 and 1936, while in the first four years of the 1930s MGs took the honours. Their high spot was the wickedly fast K3 Magnette, which had an 1 100cc six-cylinder engine with a supercharger and a Wilson preselector gearbox; the great Italian driver Tazio Nuvolari drove one to win the 1933 event.

MG, standing for 'Morris Garages' and fairly describing the derivation of parts for the early cars, became the most prolific of the popular sports car manufacturers. The first MG, built in 1923, was simply a modified Morris Oxford. By 1929 they had produced the first MG Midget, the 850cc M-type, and this was the start of a series of small, cheap to buy, uncomplicated to maintain, open two seater 'fun cars' which continued long after the War. The M gave way to the J-types, then to the PA and the bigger-engined PB, and eventually the TA.

Top: The Frazer Nash TT replica was simple versatile and unusual in retaining chain drive transmission with a separate chain for every gear

Centre: MG scored a win in the 1933 Tourist Trophy in Ulster with Nuvolari driving a supercharged K3 Magnette. Here he chases the third placed Alfa Romeo of Rose-Richards

Left: MG started mass production of cheap, simple sports cars in 1929. The cutaway drawing shows the J2 version of the Midget, produced between 1932 and 1934

MG's opposition in the 'cheap' sports car market came notably from Singer and the various hotted-up versions of the little Austin Seven: the tiny supercharged Ulster, which exceeded 100mph at Brooklands, and the milder but cheerful Nippy open two seater.

When the days of the cyclecar had passed, these Austins and other under 1 litre cars like the Morgan three-wheelers, were the smallest true sports cars on the European market. In America, naturally, sports cars were bigger—and different. Stutz had performed well at Le Mans in 1928 and their Black Hawk had finished second only to a 6½ litre Bentley. Chrysler had also done creditably in those early Le Mans years. In Grand Prix racing in the early 1920s the name of Duesenberg had become famous with Murphy's victory in the French race. Fred Duesenberg was a German-born American who had built Bugatti aero engines under licence during the First World War. In 1920 a car of his design broke the Land Speed Record and his first production car appeared, the Model A. It was an advanced design with hydraulic four wheel brakes and an overhead camshaft straight eight engine. It went well but looked ordinary, and was not a commercial success. In 1926 the company was taken over by E. L. Cord and the ambitious J and SJ Models were developed with a 6·8 litre engine. A version of the supercharged SJ, named the *Mormon Meteor* recorded 135·47mph for 24 hours in 1935. Later the same company produced two other American high performance cars, the Auburn Speedster and the front-wheel-drive Cord.

Back in Europe, what was perhaps the most outstanding sports car of

the 1930s was produced in Italy. It was the Alfa Romeo 8C2900 – the '2·9'. When the German teams swamped Grand Prix racing with money and technical know-how, Alfa found themselves unable to compete with their previously successful P3 racing cars. They had the idea of using up surplus 2·9 P3 engines – straight eights with twin superchargers giving 180bhp – in roadgoing sports cars. The 2·9 owed more than the engine to the *monoposto*; it had all-independent suspen-

sion and many other sophisticated chassis features. It was claimed to be the fastest road car of the day, though an *Autocar* contest with an 8-litre Bentley, a Delahaye, and a Talbot-Darracq failed to prove it.

The Second World War heralded the end of a sports car era. The best cars of the 1920s and 1930s had been machines of real character, often reflecting the beliefs of the men who designed and made them, with loving care and in small numbers. No wonder they are so highly prized

today. A good Bentley can fetch up to £15 000 in a British auction, and Duesenberg SJs have been valued at around the same figure. They have an aura that even the best modern sports car cannot quite capture. Perhaps then, it is not so surprising that enthusiasts are prepared to pay so much for them – and for modern replicas of Mercedes SS, Bentleys, Bugattis and SS Jaguars. They promise to bring back that certain 'something' that is exclusive to the sports cars of the Golden Era.

Sports gives way to GT

Jaguar are usually credited as being the first to bring high standards of refinement and comfort to the expected performance of a sports car, with the XK 120 which was introduced in 1948. Certainly the Coventry firm led in coupling these characteristics in a mass production model, but the trend towards the sports car in which qualities like ride, comfort, and weather protection were not sacrificed in the interests of speed started before the Second World War. Some of the large and very expensive French sports cars of the 1930s had moved in this direction, but the most significant influence came from – of all places – Germany. Since the early days the Germans had not been very interested in the stark race-bred 'traditional' sports car and their efforts in the field of fast touring cars were overshadowed by the dominance of the Hitler-financed Mercedes and Auto Union racing teams. But during the late 1930s one of the most outstanding sports cars of the era emerged – the BMW 328.

Designed by Dr Fritz Fiedler, the BMW 328 was the last development of a series of cars started in 1933. It had an advanced 2-litre six cylinder engine in an unusually rigid tubular chassis with independent front suspension. Powerful and light in weight, it had acceleration and maximum speed (100mph plus) way out of its class, coupled with fine steering and roadholding and much softer springing than was usual for a sports car. The body, an open two seater fashioned in aluminium, is the link between the square-cut

cycle-winged style of the pre-war years and the all-enveloping designs which came after. Aerodynamically efficient by the standards of the time, it had softly rounded lines with the wings flush with the bodywork. It was tremendously successful in racing in standard form but later was fitted with a variety of more streamlined all-enveloping bodies for competition. One of these, which appeared in the 1940 Mille Miglia was strikingly similar to the XK120.

After the War, BMW's Eisenach factory found itself on the Communist side of the border splitting Germany. The natural extension of the 328 theme was carried on by the Bristol Aeroplane Company when they decided to build cars in 1946. Through AFN Ltd, who had sold the 328 under the Frazer-Nash label, they bought the rights to the BMW design. The Bristol 400 saloon used the BMW chassis, and as befitted an aircraft company, had a very clean aerodynamic shape. Frazer-Nash continued to use the engine in their post-war cars, while the East Germans made a copy of the 328 called the EMW, and small companies like Veritas built cars around its components in the early 1950s.

But fewer than 500 genuine 328s were made. Jaguar were looking to the high-volume market with the XK120, which stood out as a bright star among the austerity of Earls Court at London's first post-war Motor Show. The company had previously made the SS range of cars. They made just one SS100 after the War and sold it to a garage owner in the North of England

The BMW 328 was a very advanced sports car of the 1930s, setting a theme which led to the new style which arose after the Second World War. Stirling Moss cut his motoring teeth with a 328 and is shown (right) taking part in a sporting trial in 1946, with his father as passenger. Streamlined versions of the 328 were raced in 1940 and bore a close outward resemblance to the Jaguar XK120, announced in 1948. The Jaguar did well in both racing and rallying, with Ian Appleyard its most consistently successful driver in the latter. The photograph below shows Appleyard on his way to winning a *Coupe des Alpes* in the 1950 Alpine Rally, an achievement he was to repeat with the same car – with its famous registration NUB 120 – in 1951 and 1952. A development of the XK120's twin overhead camshaft engine is still available today

called Ian Appleyard, who used it in competitions, notably the major European rallies. In 1948 he won a coveted *Coupe des Alpes* in the Alpine Rally; later, armed with an XK120 he was to score many similar successes.

The XK120 was the first mass-produced car to have a twin overhead camshaft engine. This remarkable 3 442 cc six cylinder unit, which was eventually to be enlarged to 4·2 litres, was to be the mainstay of the Jaguar range for 23 years. The new sports car had a box-section chassis with independent front suspension using torsion bar springs and a 'live'

rear axle suspended on leaf springs. It had hydraulic drum brakes all round, a four-speed gearbox and recirculating-ball type steering. The '120' referred to the car's claimed top speed, which was convincingly exceeded by a timed run in Belgium at 132·6mph in 1949, though the production version with a full-width windscreen had a maximum of around 115mph. This was at a time when only a handful of production cars could exceed 100mph. It provided this performance with a comfort, quietness and sweet-running far above that provided by most cars of its type and price. In 1948 this was

astonishingly low at £998, which perpetuated Jaguar's reputation for outstanding value-for-money high performance cars. In 1954 the XK120 was replaced by the XK140, improved in several respects over the original car, and the same theme was carried on with the XK150 series introduced in 1957. By the late 1950s the power output of the engine had been increased from 160 to 250bhp and the car's maximum speed increased to 135mph. The recirculating-ball steering had by then been replaced with the more precise rack and pinion type, while disc brakes for all four wheels were a recommended option.

More than 10 000 XK120s were sold in the United States alone. The American market was to become the most important of all for the manufacturers of performance cars. The trend towards this started with GIs returning from Europe after the War and bringing with them in large numbers one of the first available post-war sports models–the MG TC. Now the TC was neither a particularly fast nor a particularly special car, but it was cheap enough to be afforded by many young people, and from the American point-of-view represented everything a sports car should be. Low slung, with an upright radiator, separate wings and add-on head-lights, and small cutaway doors it was the antipathy of the American car of the day which was becoming ever-bigger and losing any 'personality' it ever had.

The TC was a pre-war design and as such had a beam front axle instead of independent front suspension and unfashionably large wire wheels. Its maximum speed was a modest 75mph. It was soon to be superseded by the TD which was an infinitely better car, although it did not have the same visual appeal, being based on an MG saloon chassis and having plain pressed-steel wheels. But it did have independent front suspension and rack and pinion steering, and it was faster. In due course the TD gave way to the TF, for which a 1 500cc engine was made available along with the old 1 250cc version. With a sloping radiator grille and more

flowing lines it is regarded by many to be the most attractive 'vintage style' sports car of all. In any case, it was the last of the traditional MGs, for in 1955 the firm bowed to convention by announcing the all-enveloping MGA based on a design raced at Le Mans four years before. The famous upright MG radiator had gone, to be replaced by a wide, flat token on the A's pretty body-shell. Although it gained a good reputation as a safe, reliable and enjoyable sports car, the MGA was not tremendously fast. For this reason a special Twin Cam version with a 1600cc engine and special cylinder head, producing 108bhp, was produced for sale in 1958. It had a maximum speed of 115mph and could be identified from the regular car by its perforated centre-lock wheels. The MGA Twin Cam had only a brief production run. In time the standard engine was 'bored out' to 1600cc and finally to 1800cc for the MGB, which came along in 1962, and was more modern in design yet of the timeless sort of shape that the MG team do so well.

Prior to the MGA, the post-war MG sports cars had all been called the Midget – a carry-over from the pre-war line. The name re-appeared in 1961 on a model identical to the Austin-Healey Sprite, a simple down-to-earth little car using the BMC 948cc engine of the Morris Minor. Aimed at exactly the same young people who bought the TC so eagerly a decade earlier, these two models have proved very popular in Britain.

The story of the Austin-Healey is an interesting one. Donald Healey, who had been associated with Triumph in the 1930s, became an expert at assessing the sporting opportunities of the products of the major manufacturers. He built a Riley-engined car which for a short time in the immediate post-war years could claim to be the fastest closed car on the British market. That was followed by the Healey Silverstone, a lighter competition car with narrow open bodywork and outside wings which also used the Riley 2·5 litre engine; the Nash-Healey, a rather bulky sports car with an American 3·8 litre Nash engine; and a similar car with a 3 litre

The first post-war MG, the TC (top) was based on a pre-war design and popularised the European-style sports car in America. The MG Midget lives on (above) while the recent mainstay of the marque has been the 1800cc MGB (below), production of which started in 1962. The engine is an enlarged version of that which powered the earlier MGA

Alvis engine. Neither of the latter variants were widely sold in Britain, but at the London Motor Show in 1952, Healey presented a graceful open two-seater called simply the 'Hundred'. It used a 2·6 litre four cylinder Austin saloon engine and various other proprietary parts in a simple ladder-type chassis. First gear in the saloon's normal four speed gearbox became too low to be any use in the much lighter sports car so it was blocked off, making a three-speeder which was then turned into a five-speed box by the addition of an electrically-operated overdrive unit! The Healey Hundred was well received and was adopted by Austins for production – hence the name Austin-Healey.

In time the four-cylinder engine was replaced by a six-cylinder engine of similar capacity and a four-speed gearbox with more usable ratios fitted (with overdrive as an option). This developed 102bhp, 12bhp more than the four cylinder (special versions of the earlier engine had 110 and 132bhp, for the '100M' and the '100S' respectively). In 1959 the Healey became the 3000, with a 2·9 litre engine and a drophead-

coupé body. It was a fast car—maximum 121 mph for the Mk 2 version—and gained a fine competition record, particularly in rallying, but with a chassis still essentially the same as the first car, the 'updated' Healey lost some of its appeal. Those who drove them marvelled that the factory's rally cars could stand the pounding of rough roads, for the one thing that none of the series ever had was adequate ground clearance!

In competition with the first Austin-Healey—but at a much lower price—was the Triumph TR2, also introduced in 1952. It used components from all over the Standard-Triumph range—a simple chassis frame, Triumph Mayflower suspension and a tuned version of the Standard Vanguard engine, which (in basic form) was already in use in the Morgan sports car.

The TR soon gained a reputation as a fast strong car, did well in international rallies and races and became almost standard equipment for the successful British club rally

Above: The 3000's last great ride—Timo Makinen came close to winning the 1965 RAC Rally of Great Britain with a works Austin-Healey 3000 but victory went to the Mini-Cooper driven by Aaltonen, alongside

Below: The Triumph TR2 proved a popular competition car, being fast and rugged. It achieved considerable success in rallies, particularly in Britain, and the factory entered teams in such events as the Mille Miglia. This one was driven by Gatsonides and Richardson in the 1953 event

driver. The four cylinder engine produced 100 bhp in its 1956 TR3 form, which differed only in detail from the TR2 and, coupled with the excellent Laycock overdrive, which operated on top, third and second gears (giving a choice in seven speeds in all!) could cruise at high speeds with very low engine rpm and give

surprisingly good fuel economy. The early TRs had rather skittish handling which caught a good number of owners out on a slippery road, but the *marque* will go down as one of the most successful attempts to provide a sports car that went well, was reliable and was fun to drive at a low cost. The 1956 TR3 was one of the first cars to have disc front brakes as standard. TR components were used in several specialist cars of the 1950s – the Swallow Doretti, which was nicely made but expensive and did not stay in production long, and the Peerless (later the Warwick) which was a praiseworthy but under-capitalised project to build a four seater GT car.

The low-slung, straight-sided TR2/3 body was hardly elegant but it did have a rugged appeal. In 1961, demands for more comfort and hence the need to fit winding windows, meant a new body and the end of the cutaway doors. The TR4, as the new model was called, had a less distinctive shape (it was, incidentally, based on an experimental Le Mans car of 1960) and was a less significant car, although it did have an all-synchromesh gearbox – something that was sadly lacking in other popular sports cars of the time. With ten years of production behind it, the TR chassis was becoming something of a period piece and the rather primitive independent rear suspension that came with the introduction of the TR4A in 1965 did not do much to modernise it. Still the model continued, through the TR5, when it was first fitted with the smooth and powerful six cylinder 2·5 litre Triumph engine with Lucas fuel injection – a very nice sports car power unit – and the 1969 TR6, which incorporated quite extensive changes that succeeded in giving a fresh look to the body.

Smart or soft?
Jaguar, MG, Austin-Healey and Triumph – these British models were the big selling sports cars of the 1950s. By the end of that decade the typical sports car was beginning to 'soften' a little, as more attention was paid to seating, comfort and weather protection, sometimes at the expense of traditional sports

car qualities such as responsiveness and real performance. Vintage enthusiasts could be heard to cry 'cissy' – and they still do. Such a car was the Sunbeam Alpine, a pleasant two-seater with a rather luxurious interior and a clean, stylish body that looked like a sports car even if it did not really go like one.

All but the smallest true sports cars were by this time in the 100mph-plus bracket. All had independent front suspension, most had disc brakes at the front. Very few had independent rear suspension – the beautiful but costly AC Ace was an important exception, although it used a simple transverse leaf spring arrangement. The Morgans and the Lotus Seven 'kit cars' were the only serious ones to continue with separate cycle-type wings and 'vintage'

cutaway sides. The hardtop and the purpose-built closed sports coupé were developing trends. Once again it was left to Jaguar to introduce a model to set the future scene, one which combined the more advanced ideas from racing, touring and the expensive exotic cars of Italy at a realistic price. It was an automotive milestone called the E-type.

At the time of its introduction in 1961 the E-type was as advanced as the XK120 had been 13 years before. The separate chassis of the XK series had gone, to be replaced by a

Below: The Jaguar E-type was intended for the road but was raced extensively. Graham Hill drove this lightweight version to victory over Mike Parkes' Ferrari GTO at Silverstone. in 1963

Bottom: Sophisticated GT – the famous 'gull wing' Mercedes 300SL

Top: Mercedes moved away from the race-bred GT towards a new style of luxury fast touring car combining good roadholding with a comfortable ride. It started as the 230SL and by 1968 had become the 2·8 litre 280SL

Above: Beautiful simplicity of line—the Lancia Aurelia, which followed unorthodox traditions

stressed-steel unit structure not unlike that of the racing D-type which it resembled. The front suspension was also D-type-inspired, while at the rear there was a new independent system using four coil springs. Disc brakes were fitted all round. The E-type was over 4cwt lighter than the XK150 it replaced, and with 265bhp from the 3·8 litre engine its performance was fantastic: 150mph maximum speed with 0–60mph time of 7 seconds and 0–100 in just over 16 seconds. These figures were not just the best for a car in its class,

they were among the best for any car at any price. And the E-type looked marvellous too, both in its open, convertible form and as a 'fastback' fixed-head coupé. Jaguar had set new standards for roadgoing sports cars and co-incidentally provided a good example of the growing breed of 'Grand Tourers'.

The GT car is no more easy to define than the sports car. The term has come to apply to closed cars, usually, although not always with four seats, and rarely with the same comfort in the back as in the front. The *berlinetta* bodies of Italian coachbuilders, notably on early Ferraris, were really the beginning of this trend, although some cars of similar layout had appeared in the late 1930s. The 1954 Mercedes 300SL—which was also in every

sense a proper sports car–can be considered another early GT. It was developed from the cars that raced in 1952 and won Le Mans that year; it might never have gone into production at all had the US importer not guaranteed to sell 1000 300SLs.

The 300SL had a light multi-tubular chassis, an all synchromesh gearbox and a fuel-injected engine which produced 240bhp from 3 litres –a very high output for the time. The 'gull wing' coupé body of this car provided great comfort to go with the sparkling performance. The 300SL was billed as the fastest production car in the world, with a top speed just short of 150mph. The 'gull wing' was replaced in 1957 by a roadster which was much less exciting to look at but did incorporate better rear suspension to replace the simple swing-axle independent system which had made the coupé's handling unpredictable and given it a reputation as a difficult car to drive fast. The 190SL, which was announced at the same time as the 300 and looked quite similar, was a nicely appointed sporting touring car rather than a true sports car. The successor to both these cars was the 230SL of 1963, an unusual blend of luxury and sporting characteristics which set some trends of its own. It proved that good roadholding could be combined with soft springing and a limousine-smooth ride, and adopted a very wide track for its size. This produced a wide, flat look that was later to become fashionable.

But the real masters of the *Gran Turismo* style were the Italians. Aside from the Ferraris and Maseratis which were (and still are) very expensive and often produced on a one-off basis, Lancia and Alfa Romeo manufactured very good examples of this breed throughout the 1950s and 1960s. Lancia's Aurelia, which first appeared in the early 1950s was the epitome of the GT of the period. A coupé with splendidly simple lines and a sloping 'fastback' tail, it also had a very good performance and became very popular transport for motoring personalities and drivers of the time, Juan Manuel Fangio, Mike Hawthorn and Jean Behra among them. The Aurelia had a V6 engine of 2½ litres capacity, with the gearbox mounted, rather unusually, in unit with the differential rather than the engine. The front suspension was independent by a sliding pillar system and at the rear De Dion suspension with inboard rear brakes was used on later models. Lancia were pioneers in the what is known as integral chassis where the body structure is so designed as to take the place of a separate chassis (this system is used for most mass-production saloons). The larger Flaminia, made in saloon and GT coupé forms, was only slightly more conventional and had several of the refreshingly 'different' characteristics of the older car.

In 1960 Lancia announced the Flavia saloon as their new basic model, with front wheel drive and a new horizontally-opposed four cylinder engine. The saloon was far from pretty, but the coupé version by the great designer Pininfarina was simply beautiful and, like its predecessor ten years before, set the visual standards for the GT type.

By the mid-1950s Alfa Romeo had given up racing, when their pre-war Grand Prix design was finally beaten by the other great Italian marque,

Ferrari. After the complicated extravagance of cars like the pre-war '2·9', the Milanese firm entered the smaller car market and made a very versatile little twin-cam four-cylinder engine which powered everything from the Giulietta Sprint Veloce coupé to the firm's front-wheel drive Romeo van! There was a 2 litre Alfa in these days too, but the Giulietta, a classically proportioned little car in its coupé form, was the trend setter. It was quiet-running, had good steering and handling and was quite softly sprung – it had many of the better attributes of the 'soft' semi-sports cars of the early 1960s, coupled with a performance that was very good for its size. Looking at the valued characteristics of today's sports cars, it was ahead of its time. In due course the 1300cc engine was enlarged, a five speed gearbox became standard and a new Bertone coupé body came along, which also proved to be a significant and long-lasting design.

Even before the E-type, Britain had candidates in the GT category. The AC Aceca, the good-looking coupé version of the Ace qualified, though it was only a two seater, so did Allard's Jaguar-engined coupé, the Jensen and the various developments of the Bristol. But the British GT champion in those years was undoubtedly Aston Martin. They built the two/four seater DB coupé just after the War, raced it at Le Mans and elsewhere and used the experience gained to develop and refine the model over the years. Mechanically, the DB2 and its successor, the Mark 3, were fairly conventional and unremarkable, save for the strong twin overhead camshaft engine developed from a unit designed by W. O. Bentley for Lagonda immediately before the War. The DB4, which caused a tremendous stir when it was announced in 1958, was in truth, little more advanced, though it used a light-alloy engine and disc brakes on all four wheels. Reasonably light for its size at 26 cwt it provided a good performance and a 140mph maximum speed, but the most striking thing about it was the body. The slightly awkward humped back of the DB Mark 3 was replaced by one with a

The Aston Martin DB4 was a stylish, high-performance coupé in what is now known as 'two plus two' style and was much praised at the time of its introduction in 1958. A DB4GT version was subsequently offered with more power, a shorter wheelbase and some bodywork changes; this was entered in sports car races, as here at Goodwood driven by Innes Ireland

very graceful sloping roof which co-incidentally gave it room for four 'proper' seats. It looked like an Italian thoroughbred – which in fact was what it was, for the body was designed in Italy. The theme of this car was continued until the DBS shape replaced the DB6 in 1968, though none of the succeeding models retained the elegance of line of the DB4.

The surprising thing about the Aston Martin and its Continental competitors like Ferrari and Maserati was how old-fashioned they were from a technical point of view. They had marvellous engines with lots of cylinders and camshafts and prodigious power outputs, but in 1961 only the Mercedes 300SL had independent rear suspension and that of a design which was markedly inferior to that of the E-type Jaguar. They were opulent, luxurious carriages for the young-at-heart wealthy and their significance was that they incorporated luxury-car items within a sporting framework. Power steering was to come – even to Ferraris – while for the American market such cars were already being fitted with air-conditioning units.

Automatic transmission could be fitted to these cars, too, if the customer wanted it. America, the home of the modern style of 'automatic', had set that trend in the early 1950s. The Chevrolet Division of General Motors, noting the success of European sports cars in America, decided to build one themselves. They called it the Corvette. It used parts from the GM saloon ranges, including a 160bhp six cylinder engine – and a two-speed automatic transmission. It had to have that because, even in those days, the fitting of automatic transmission in American cars was so widespread that GM did not have a suitable manual gearbox available. But the Corvette did break new ground in another direction – it had a glass-fibre body. This moulded plastic construction was chosen because GM did not expect to sell enough of the cars to justify the great expense of setting up the equipment to make complex metal panels. The model turned out to be a bigger success

Corvette evolution. A racing special (left) built by GM styling chief Bill Mitchell as a private venture led to the shape for the Corvette Stingray (right) which replaced the more garish earlier Chevrolet model in 1963

than they expected but the plastic bodywork became very much a part of the Corvette concept and was retained for subsequent models.

Plastics make perfect

Nowadays glass-fibre is the recognised method of body construction for small manufacturers building cars at a relatively low price. It has

Glass-fibre bodywork allowed Marcos to produce this spectacularly shaped coupé which used Volvo or Ford engines. For many years Marcos used wooden chassis construction

several advantages: it does not rust or decay, it is light and strong and it can quite easily be repaired – and the manufacturer makes a great saving on tooling costs. When production rises to the 30 000 level, achieved with the Corvette by 1970, this cost advantage over metal construction becomes marginal. But in Britain in the 1950s little companies sprang up all over the place offering stylish – and sometimes not so stylish – glass-fibre bodies to turn your aged Austin Seven or upright Ford 10 into a racy-looking sports car (few of them in fact turned out that way because the original cars' wheels rarely fitted the image). This was

the forerunner of the beach buggy fad, offering a similar promise to worn-out Volkswagens. Some of these companies became car manufacturers in their own right, but most subsequently disappeared.

A few specialist firms arose from the opposite direction, as it were. They had built cars, usually for competition, and glass-fibre body construction gave them the chance of putting their ambitious ideas into production. Among these cars were the Triumph TR-engined Peerless, the Elva, the TVR—who continue with their pretty little coupé today—and the Marcos (which started life with an incredibly ugly car made largely of wood, later replaced by a very futuristic glass-fibre covering for the plywood chassis).

By far the most significant of these small enthusiastic companies was Lotus. Colin Chapman started making Lotus 'specials' in a stable in a London suburb in 1952. He competed in trials and in races with them and before long it was clear that he was to become one of the great innovators among car designers of the post-war era. His cars, characterised by their combina-tion of light weight, excellent road-holding and good aerodynamics, won races the world over. When he came to develop the Elite GT coupé for production, he elected to use glass-fibre, but in typical Chapman style was not content to use it just for the bodywork—he built a saloon-car style integral body/chassis out of plastic which gave the car a tremendous weight advantage (it weighed only 13cwt) and a superb performance for a car of its modest 1220cc engine capacity. For various reasons, the beautiful Elite was not entirely satisfactory as a Grand Tourer, although it did very well in racing. Chapman went back to a steel chassis for subsequent Lotuses, but he continued to use glass-fibre bodywork and remains convinced that it is ideal for the purpose.

Longer established British manufacturers have also used glass-fibre. Jensen were early pioneers with the Austin-engined 541 and only gave it up when they moved into the more

The Lotus Elite was a significant design, utilising a glass-fibre monocoque construction. It was succeeded by the Elan, shown in the cutaway drawing, which had a steel backbone chassis and a glass-fibre body. It set new standards in roadholding

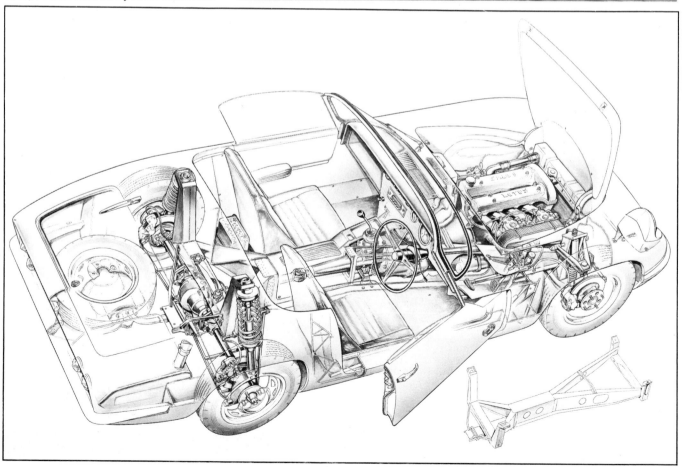

Just before the start of the first post-war Le
Mans 24-hour Race, in 1949. The largest-
engined cars in the entry head the line-up for
the traditional 'run and jump' start. Number 6
is the 4¼ litre Bentley saloon entered by
H. S. F. Hay, which finished sixth in the race,
while the first five cars are French—two
Talbots, two Delahayes, and the Delettrez
diesel (number 5). The race was won by
Luigi Chinetti and Lord Selsdon with a
supercharged 2 litre Ferrari

Left: Stirling Moss has been described as the
'greatest driver never to win the World
Championship', and although his
performances at Le Mans were consistently
good, he did not win the 24-hour race either.
In 1953 he drove this Jaguar C-type to
second place, partnered by Peter Walker. The
similar team car driven by Tony Rolt and
Duncan Hamilton won the race

'On the limit' testing with a Jensen FF—the first sporting car to be offered with four-wheel drive. Jensen made a limited number of these cars alongside the outwardly similar Interceptor coupé until 1972. The extra expense and complexity was rewarded by surefootedness in slippery conditions

luxurious class with the Chrysler-engined Interceptor and four wheel drive FF. A more surprising model to be thus clothed was the Daimler SP250, which this previously rather sedate company launched in 1959. Scarcely attractive to look at, the SP250, also briefly known as the Dart, had a nice lightweight V8 2½ litre engine. The model had only a short production life (which included a batch for British police forces) before Jaguar, who had acquired the company, axed it; the V8 engine was later offered in a Jaguar saloon body.

There is more to be said about the Chevrolet Corvette, which in its original form was pretty awful; a sports car only in its fashion-conscious looks. But, to their credit, GM decided to persevere with it, remaining alone among the big American manufacturers in offering an entirely home-grown sports car. Developments improved the Corvette immeasurably. It gained V8 engines of various sizes and power outputs, a three-speed gearbox, then a new four-speed manual gearbox. In 1963 it underwent a major change with a spectacular new body derived from a special racing Corvette called the Sting Ray and mechanical improvements like better steering and independent rear suspension, which in some ways was not unlike the E-type's but used a transverse leaf spring. In 1968 a new

and more graceful body was introduced, cleverly incorporating the same Sting Ray theme. By then it had become a comfortable, high performance, and generally very satisfactory sports car – even by European standards.

The big, rumbling V8
Chevrolet's use of a powerful V8 engine in such a relatively small and light car in the late 1950s was the signal for a burst of new thinking about the sports car applications for these rugged and reliable American power units. The idea of installing one in a European style sports car chassis began to look distinctly attractive: because of their large capacities these engines produced plenty of power without the need for sophisticated valve gear and carburation that made European high performance cars complex and expensive. This, of course, was the idea behind Briggs Cunningham's Le Mans cars, Lance Reventlow's Scarab sports/racers, and the successful early post-war products of Allard, who used Ford, Chrysler and Cadillac engines to obtain very impressive performance from quite primitive chassis. But somehow the

idea did not spread as it might have done. The big American engines did not have the much-coveted 'sporting' characteristics. They were mostly heavy, and thus threatened to upset the balance of a chassis. They had generous torque, making the gearbox almost unnecessary. The sports car enthusiast took pride in nicely-timed gearchanges to match the 'peaky' characteristics of his highly-tuned engine. The lazy V8s sounded coarse – loud but rumbling; no comparison with the shrill note of a high-revving small capacity straight-four or 'six'.

In the newly emergent large GT car, with its accent on comfort and smooth running, these characteristics could be accepted willingly, but before that happened the AC Cobra appeared. This was in no way a smooth refined gentleman's carriage; it was a blood-and-thunder sports car in the old tradition.

The Cobra was the idea of Carroll Shelby, a tall Texan with a cowboy hat and a big smile who raced in Europe in the late 1950s and had a Le Mans win with Aston Martin to his credit. In 1961 he started making enquiries around the Detroit car makers about the supply of high performance engines. General Motors had a marvellous aluminium V8 (the one that eventually became a Rover, and was used in their saloons and the Morgan) but they were not keen to supply. Ford, however, were just at the point of planning a programme to improve their performance 'image' and Shelby was able to do a deal with them.

He had chosen his chassis: the venerable AC Ace. Eight years old, this was a fast and advanced car at the time of its introduction, with all-independent suspension and a shapely body looking very much like the 1949 Le Mans Ferrari and the British Tojeiro-Bristol on which its design was based. During its life it had been fitted with the old AC engine, the Bristol unit and latterly the Ford Zephyr six cylinder.

Shelby joined the brash 4·2 litre Ford V8 to AC's classic British sports car, fitted an American four-speed gearbox and some wide wheels and tyres, and *voila!* – he had built a

The AC Cobra—an Anglo-American hybrid by Carroll Shelby using the old AC Ace chassis and a big US Ford V8 engine. In time the car's suspension was modernised, bigger engines and automatic transmission were offered and special racing coupés built

production American hot rod!

Ford took Shelby under their corporate wing and used the Cobra for their first tentative steps into long distance sports car racing, which eventually were to lead to the Le Mans winning GT40 project. The demands of racing led to various streamlined coupé versions of the Cobra, one of which hit the headlines in England when, it was alleged, it was tested early one morning on the M1 motorway at over 180mph. Some time later the Ace's old-fashioned leaf spring suspension was replaced by coil springs with a new layout designed at Ford and the 355bph 7-litre Ford engine was also made available.

Naturally others followed the Shelby lead. TVR were early emulators with the fearsome Griffith, a version of which was raced in British club events and called the Mongoose—because it ate Cobras! The Sunbeam distributor in California commissioned Shelby to instal a Ford V8 in an Alpine. The Rootes Group (in its pre-Chrysler days) approved, and the car went into production as the Sunbeam Tiger. It was just what the 'soft' Alpine needed—some guts to go with its pleasantly appointed interior—and made it into an excellent touring sports car. Somehow it never gained quite the reputation it deserved.

Many luxury GT cars gained American power, at less cost and sometimes more convenience than the fussy race-bred engines of their competitors. In Britain Bristol and Jensen adopted Chrysler V8s, while among the Continental exotics, Iso and De Tomaso used Chevrolet and Ford respectively and the Swiss Monteverdi had Chrysler power.

To push or to pull?

To this point the cars discussed in this chapter have almost all been of conventional front engine-rear drive

Ferry Porsche (right), son of Ferdinand Porsche with the prototype of the 356 series of Porsche cars built in 1948. At first these cars made use of running gear and engines from the Volkswagen Beetle but in time all VW derivation disappeared

type and it is to this format that the traditional sports car has grown up. But there are other ways of solving the problem of making a car which is fast, compact, handles well and provides adequate passenger and luggage space. An obvious step is to put the engine next to the wheels that it drives, therefore eliminating the need for a propeller shaft running from the front of the car to the back. That was the simple theory behind the Volkswagen, the most successful 'economy' car of all time. The VW also had an air-cooled engine and simple independent rear suspension by swing-axles. It was designed by Dr Ferdinand Porsche and when after the War his son Ferry set up a business to build cars under their family name it was natural that they should carry out long-held plans for a VW-based sports car.

Thus the first Porsche, in 1948, was an open two seater which used a rear-mounted 1 100cc VW engine, as well as transmission, suspension and steering from the 'People's Car'. A coupé body followed, and continued with only small modifications throughout the life of this '356' Porsche series. Thanks to the good wind-cheating shape of the body it gave a very good performance and fuel economy from its modest power unit, which was eventually enlarged to 1 300cc, 1 500cc and then 1 600cc.

The Jaguar C-type was a special version of the XK120 road car, with a tubular chassis, a streamlined body and a more powerful engine. The cockpit (above) was stark, but the car was a true two-seater. The famous XK twin-cam six-cylinder engine was further developed for the D-type (right), which first appeared in 1954, and it powered all Jaguar road cars until the advent of the V12 in 1971

The Ferrari 225 was a contemporary of the Jaguar C-type. This 1952 car was a development of the model which won the 1949 Le Mans race, and it was also raced with considerable success. The cockpit (above) contrasts with the Jaguar's in having a simple painted panel, of the type common in more mundane cars of the period. The long gear lever actuates a five-speed gearbox. The engine (left) is a classic Ferrari V12, of 2·7 litres, which produced 210bhp at 7200rpm

Early Porsches had a very bad reputation for wagging their tails in a manner which was difficult to control – this oversteer was a penalty of the swing axle layout, as well as the engine location which concentrated a lot of weight in the tail. Other firms might have abandoned such a layout when they became established – or might not have used it in the first place – but Porsche carried on with the rear-mounted air-cooled engines (to this day) and swing-axles (until the 911 series came along in 1963). They succeeded in improving the car's behaviour and gained a tremendous reputation for the engineering and finish of their product. The 911, a smooth, 'two plus two' coupé of tremendous performance and good road manners, rates as one of the best all-round sports/GT cars on the market; by 1971 it had a 2·4 litre engine and in its 911S form was capable of 143mph.

Few sports car manufacturers have followed Porsche's rear-engined example, and those who did usually did so because they were making use of chassis components from rear-engined saloons. This applied to Abarth, the Italian tuning wizard, who achieved some phenomenal power outputs from little Fiat engines and fitted some very attractive coupé bodies around them. Derivatives of the small rear-engined Renault saloons were also popular in France and one of them, the Alpine, was adopted some years after its introduction by the State-owned French company for their factory bid in European rallies. It did exceedingly well and won the 1971 Constructors' Rally Championship as well as premier events like the Monte Carlo Rally. In a way, however, this was because of, rather than in spite of, the 'tail-happy' handling which such rear-heavy cars can provide. The ability to 'hang the tail out' is a big advantage on the loose-surfaced roads found in rallies, while more precise progress pays off on the race track.

Partly for handling reasons and partly because of space considerations, the rear-engined small saloons had largely given way to front wheel drive designs by the onset of

the 1970s. British manufacturers had been among the first to use this arrangement in a popular small car with the Austin and Morris Minis, which later became so highly tuned that they became sports cars in their own right. These front-drive cars had a surefootedness that the rear-engined Continental saloons could never give, they scooted round corners almost as if they were on rails, and packaging the engine and transmission together in the front of the car left the back free for luggage and people. But for mainstream sports and GT cars front-wheel-drive had few adherents. The understeer characteristic (tendency to go straight on 'at the limit') of front wheel drive cars is not really in keeping with sports car style and the arrangement presents problems in achieving a low bonnet line and dictates a rather differently shaped car. But Lancia did make a superbly elegant GT from their Flavia saloon in the early 1960s, and its younger brother the V4 Fulvia coupé became a highly successful rally car, culminating in the Italian firm winning the Constructors' Championship in 1972. Another successful rallying firm, Saab from Sweden, produced a little two seater sports version of their basic saloon for some years, called the Sonett. It has been sold mainly in the United States.

A question of balance

But while rear engines and front wheel drive had their applications

In 1972 Porsche announced the largest-yet engine for the 911, a 2·7 litre unit in the Carrera RS. With aerodynamic spoilers front and rear, it is fast and handles well. This Carrera won the 1973 Daytona 24 hours.

for road cars, those designed specifically for racing have since the early 1960s almost exclusively used the mid-engined layout. Pioneered in single seater racing by the pre-war Auto Unions and after the War by Cooper, and in sports car racing by Porsche (whose competition cars had their engines *ahead* of the rear axle), it was a logical layout for the lightweight racing car. Mounting the engine behind the driver allowed a lower, more aerodynamic shape and could lead to a near perfect front-to-rear weight balance within compact dimensions, giving better handling and roadholding. It was inevitable that in time the mid-engined concept would be applied to everyday road cars.

Credit for being the first to offer these racing principles in a modern production roadgoing sports car should go to René Bonnet, who had been the 'B' of DB, a small company which made the tiny cars that used to do so well in the small capacity classes at Le Mans. Bonnet designed the Djet, a rather humpty-backed two-seater coupé with an 1100cc Renault engine mounted just behind the driver. In 1964 the firm was acquired by the Matra aerospace firm as their first move in the automobile field, a venture which was to lead to wins in the World Championship and at Le Mans. The Djet became a Matra-Bonnet and was eventually replaced by the Matra 530, a most curious looking car with a German Ford V4 engine mounted amidships. The latter was to prove somewhat embarrassing when Matra came to a marketing agreement with the French Chrysler subsidiary!

At the other end of the scale, Ford sold a few detuned GT40 racers for use on the road. But the next development from a pure road car point of view came from a rather surprising area. The firm of Lamborghini had started building powerful and expensive GT cars with a new V12 engine in 1963 and when production of these front-engined cars was properly under way, they teased the motoring world with a rather unusual chassis displayed at the 1965 Turin Motor Show. It had the same glorious V12 engine, but with an important difference – it was mounted transversely across the chassis behind the driver, with the five-speed gearbox behind it. By the following Spring it had been clothed with a dramatic ultra-low coupé body and named the Miura. It was, in many ways, the ultimate sports car of the time and certainly one of the fastest, capable of over 170mph in its later 'S' form. Other 'exotic' car specialists followed Lamborghini's lead. Ferrari first applied the principle to the Dino coupé, based on a sports/racing car and initially offered with a 2 litre and then a 195bhp 2·4 litre V6 engine which it shared with the conventional Fiat model of the same name. In the Ferrari Dino the engine was also transversely mounted. When produced in quantity this Dino turned out to be competitive in price with the more expensive Porsches, thus opening up a new, cheaper market for Ferrari. Fast, beautiful to look at and immensely satisfying to drive, the Dino is regarded by many to be the ultimate in small sports cars.

In Britain, Lotus were early in the mid-engined market with the Europa, a low glass fibre bodied coupé with racing-style reclining driving position and very high standards of roadholding in the Lotus fashion. As always, Colin

Lamborghini's Supercar. The Miura S had a 430bhp 4-litre V12 mounted transversely behind the driver, and a top speed of 170mph. The body was designed by Bertone

Chapman had been clever. He took the front wheel drive Renault 16 engine and gearbox and turned them round so that they fitted in the back of the Europa. For the first two years of its life the Europa was sold only for export but subsequently it was offered in England in component form and then as a revised model with the Ford-Lotus Twin Cam engine.

Porsche did something similar when they became reunited with Volkswagen to produce the 914 series in 1969. This was an attempt to bring Porsches to a wider audience and the basic version had a VW engine and running gear while there was the option (914/6) of a Porsche engine and components giving a lot more performance at a proportionally higher price. Both engines are horizontally-opposed in cylinder layout so the 914 could have a shallow luggage compartment above the engine, as well as at the front. It uses a development of the earlier Porsche 'Targa' roof idea, substituting a detachable glass-fibre panel for a hood, mounted at the windscreen rail and on a strong roll-protection hoop at the rear, and stowable in the luggage bay. Similar arrangements were offered for the Chevrolet Corvette and the Matra 530.

The VW-Porsche is perhaps the most practical mid-engined design

The Fiat X1/9 is a practical mid-engined sports car, although as the drawing shows this layout imposes space limitations

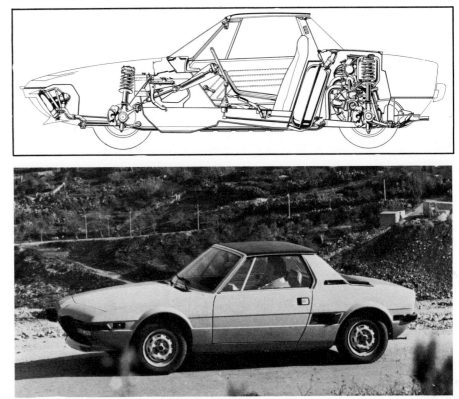

The Chevrolet Division of General Motors was
an early large-scale user of glass fibre for
sports car bodywork with the original
Corvette, a model which matured through the
first Sting Ray (see page 31) to the more
shapely design of the late 1960s. This is a
1971 convertible; an alternative version with
removable roof panels and a roll-over bar
proved more popular

Contrasting Lotuses. The Europa (above) was among the first mid-engined production cars. Initially fitted with a Renault engine, it was subsequently offered with the Ford-Lotus Twin Cam engine used in the successful Elan (left), a small, light and nimble front-engined two-seater. Luggage space in the Europa is restricted to rather small compartments front and rear

to date, but it still suffers from space problems. There is, for example, nowhere to put your jacket should you decide to take it off and the passenger seat is occupied. The author remembers watching the drivers of the first 914/6 to appear on the RAC Rally trying in vain to find somewhere to stow crash helmets, maps and the other paraphernalia a rally crew needs. There is no room for the seat backs to recline – a feature which has made many GT coupés such comfortable long-distance touring and rally cars. The VW-Porsche has an air-cooled engine and a rather unattractive boxy front. When there is the need to accommodate a water radiator and find somewhere to store the spare wheel in a lower, more stylish nose, one possible luggage area is completely filled. The temptation to make the car ultra-low and retain a smooth attractive shape also creates visibility problems – particularly to the rear – and steeply raked windscreens can increase temperatures in tight-fitting cockpits to an unbearably high level on a hot day.

So while the mid-engined sports car is gaining ground and is an important link between road sports cars and racing design (and the consequent improvements in road holding and handling), it has not become the standard layout for all sports and GT cars. It may never do so. One snag from a manufacturing point of view is that midships engines cannot have a widespread application for cars with more than one row of seats, and popular sports cars tend to be built around components from the bigger-selling saloon car lines. On the other hand, the trend in small saloons towards front wheel drive has produced some very compact transverse engine-transmission units which can be installed equally well at the rear, as Fiat have shown with their ingenious XI/9 128 Spider.

Conventional sophistication

The developments of recent years in the field of tyre (especially the radial-ply type) and suspension design have vastly improved the standards of roadholding, ride and handling that can be achieved with the conventional layouts that the most popular

Top: The VW-Porsche 914 is boxy, but more practical than most mid-engined cars. It was first made available with either a Porsche or a VW engine

Above: The first Datsun sports car to be sold abroad was the SPL310 Fairlady

sports and GT cars still retain.

Lotus set some of the standards with the successor to the Elite – the Elan – introduced in 1963. It was a small, lightweight open two-seater using a simple but strong backbone chassis frame and a glass fibre body. The engine was basically a Ford four cylinder with a twin overhead camshaft cylinder head made specially for Lotus. It was fast (0–60 mph in 8½ seconds and 115 mph top speed) but its real advance was in its suspension, which provided a soft and comfortable ride with fantastic roadholding and very precise handling. Four years later Lotus brought out a 'stretched' Elan called

the +2, which accommodated two small rear seats within a larger body. By then the Jaguar E-type was also available in a (very) occasional four-seater form on a longer-wheelbase chassis, which, coincidentally, allowed automatic transmission to be offered. Far more sports and GT cars offered such an option, including Porsche, who attempted to give the best of both manual and automatic transmission with the Sportomatic, which used a normal gearlever but incorporated the clutch into switches in the gearlever knob.

The fixed-head GT coupé has become increasingly popular. The MGB had been made available with such a body style in 1965 and was a big success, both commercially and aesthetically. Triumph produced a similar 'hatchback' called the GT6, using a bigger engine in the chassis of the small Spitfire. Reliant, a

British firm previously known for their three-wheelers, who had done well with their Ford Zephyr-engined and glass fibre bodied Scimitar, endeavoured to combine some of the advantages of an estate car into a GT (with fold-down rear seats giving a large rear luggage bay). They called it the GTE and it became their staple model. Volvo copied them with a new version of the old P1800 coupé in 1971.

But the big success story in the GT market in the late 1960s came from Japan. Datsun, who had made an uninspiring two seater called the Fairlady in 1963, came back six years later with the 240Z coupé. They had done their homework well. The 240Z was a racy looking sports car with ample room for two and their luggage, a beefy 150bhp six cylinder overhead camshaft engine and the option of a five speed gearbox. It offered equipment previously confined to much more expensive cars at a price, in America at least, comparable to the British TRs and MGs. It was hardly surprising that demand far exceeded supply and it was not long before the Datsun became the world's best selling sports car, mainly on the strength of its American sales. It was well received in Europe too, and competed with distinction in tough road events like the East African Safari.

MG, Triumph, Austin-Healey and Jaguar were by this time part of British Leyland. The Austin-Healey disappeared, but it was not long before the name Healey appeared on a sports car again, this time coupled with Jensen in a venture financed by California motor trader Kjell Qvale. The Jensen-Healey is in the Healey tradition of using parts from all over the industry – Vauxhall Viva suspension, a Chrysler gearbox and a twin-overhead camshaft all-aluminium four cylinder engine made by Lotus. Although conventional in layout, the 140bhp 2 litre Lotus power unit gives it performance figures second only to the Lotus Elan in its class.

Aston Martin marketed a new 5·3 litre V8 engine for the DBS, while experiencing financial trouble. Jaguar announced their long-awaited V12 in 1971. This was also a big engine – 5·3 litres – and a complicated one to be provided in cars which were still extremely good value for money (the E-type and later the Jaguar XJ12 saloon). But although it is an amazingly quiet and smooth power unit, it does not have the sporting characteristics of the old race-bred XK, and it turned the E-type – by now a more weighty car with rather cluttered lines – into a quiet, refined GT which was not as fast in outright speed as the original six-cylinder car and only slightly quicker in acceleration, despite the extra 100bhp given by the V12.

The V12 Jaguar engine did however have methods to control its exhaust emissions built into the design and this was an important feature when some manufacturers were having to withdraw their higher performance engines from the American market because they could not meet – or their low production did not justify modifying them to meet – ever more stringent government regulations. The United States safety rules were also having a widespread effect. Hence the massive bumpers of the Jensen-Healey, the pliable nose section of the 1973 Corvette and the general reduction in the number of convertibles.

The fast, well mannered and comfortable Grand Touring car, exotic and futuristic in its most expensive form, and almost saloon-like in the lower price bracket, had taken the place of the rorty, traditional sports car. For the manufacturers – and many customers – it was quite simply a more practical proposition.

Below: The Jensen-Healey follows traditional sports car ideas and incorporates a mixture of proprietary components

Bottom: The elegant Aston Martin DBS gained an all-aluminium 5·4 litre V8 in 1969

Rallying sports cars. Datsun have achieved success with the 240Z in the tougher events, notably the East African Safari; the photograph (opposite) shows Rauno Aaltonen and Paul Easter during the 1973 Monte Carlo Rally. Alpine started the trend to racing-type lightweight cars for classic rallies. The Renault-engined Tour de France *Berlinette* won the Monte Carlo Rally in 1971 and 1973. The top photograph shows Jean-Pierre Nicolas negotiating the *Col de Turini*. Porsche did very well in rallies with the 911, winning the Monte three times. (Left: Bjorn Waldegaard's winning car being serviced during the 1970 rally). Fiat entered into a full programme with a modified version of the 124 Spider, above, which won the Acropolis and Austrian Alpine rallies in 1972

A Modern Glimpse of Yesterday

You look through a flat, shallow windscreen. It has a fairly substantial frame but there's no visibility problem; to the sides there is clear, unimpeded vision—and fresh air. The narrow engine cover stretches out ahead, its centre hinge forming an 'aiming line' to the tapering nose. It is curiously practical that bonnet—engine-shaped if you consider it—with two parallel rows of louvres to let the heat out and some air in. The plain nose cowling, aside from its gentle slope, reflects the radiator within. The front wheels are covered by equally simple wings—mud-guards to catch mud and rain, and provide a mounting for the side-lights, no more, no less—extended back to form a step alongside those little cutaway doors; a 'running board'. The back? All it has to do is contain the fuel tank, spare wheel and the rear lamps. The 'spare' fits in an indentation in an otherwise straight panel; it's proud to be there, with no attempt at concealment. The steering wheel is close, upright, the seat doesn't adjust and it is not entirely comfortable. But the stubby little gear lever falls nicely to hand. That instrument panel is a bit stark, but tells you most of what you want to know. The rev counter is right there in front of you, through the wheel. The speedometer? Oh, that's in front of the passenger. Let her worry—or even be impressed by it.

Such a description could fit dozens of cars of the 1920s and 1930s. It could apply to a smaller number in the 1940s and 1950s. But in the Sophisticated Seventies it can mean only one thing—a Morgan.

Yet a Morgan isn't a replica, like the fine but fake Bugattis, Mercedes and what-have-yous that crop up from time to time. It is a direct, linear descendant of a car that first appeared in 1936. It is modern in the sense that it has an up-to-date power unit, a very competitive performance, disc brakes, radial-ply tyres and good lighting, and has even passed the crash tests required before a car can be sold in America. It is distinctly old fashioned in the way it looks, the way it is made and the way it rides over bad roads.

It is not that the Morgan family (the firm's founder H. F. S. Morgan died in 1959 and his son Peter is now the boss) are particularly stubborn. They have never been keen for their company—situated in the Malvern Link in rural Worcestershire and currently employing around 100 people—to grow big. As a result they have never found it necessary to go out and research the car market, to build the sort of car that people *say*

they want. The Morgan is not like that, it is a no-compromise car; you either love it or hate it. Enough people love it to keep production flowing at a steady nine or ten a week, and for there to be a substantial waiting list, even today.

The present models outwardly differ surprisingly little from that first Morgan four-wheeler of 1936. While MG (altogether in a bigger league than Morgan) gradually developed a similar theme until under the British Motor Corporation they produced their first all-enveloping body on the MGA, Morgan stopped at the point reached by the Abingdon's firm's TF model of 1954/5. Several years later, in 1963, they did dabble with a glass fibre all-enveloping coupé body for a model called the Plus Four Plus, but one suspects that they were never entirely happy

Morgan are alone now in offering for sale a traditional four seater open sports car, a style which was very popular in the 1920s and 1930s. This is the 1600cc Ford engined 4/4

Above: 3½ litres in a traditional framework—the Plus 8

Left: Plus 4 Super Sports at Le Mans. The Plus Four Plus coupé (below) had a short life

with it and only 49 were made before the idea was quietly dropped.

All Morgans to this day use the same type of sliding-pillar coil spring independent front suspension that first appeared on the spidery little single seat three wheeler that 'H.F.S.' built in 1909. This was the age of the cyclecar, which meant a vehicle with a chassis weight of less than 770lbs and an engine of less than 1100cc. Some of the examples of this rather rudimentary breed of early motor car were single seaters, others carried a passenger ahead or behind the driver and still others had conventional, if tight, side-by-side seating. The latter was the path Morgan elected to take when popular demand led him to produce cars for sale. Morgan successfully stuck with the three-wheeler concept long after most of their competitors had given it up. The Morgan Runabout, as it was first called, was fast and did well in competition. In 1925 a special streamlined model was timed over a kilometre at 104·68mph, making it officially the fastest unsupercharged car in the world. Five years later a racing model took the One Hour record at over 100mph.

Generation gap. The Morgan Plus 8 stands alongside a fine example of the Morgan 'trike'—a 1934 JAP-engined Super Sports. This had an 1100cc vee-twin cylinder engine producing 40bhp, giving the three wheeler weighing only 8cwt a spirited performance

Many different types of engine were used in the Morgan 'trike' over the years, usually derived from motorcycles. In 1933 a 4 cylinder Ford engine was fitted and the three-wheeler remained so powered until it finally ceased production in 1950.

The four-wheeler, designated the 4/4 to indicate that it had four wheels and four cylinders, was first powered by 1100cc Coventry Climax engine. A special version of the 1267cc Standard 9 engine followed this and was used until the need for more power brought in the 2 litre Standard Vanguard engine in 1950. This much faster version was called the Plus Four. In due course the more highly tuned engine of the Triumph TR2 took the Vanguard unit's place and a second series of 4/4 using the side-valve 1172cc Ford 10 engine was introduced. For racing there was an aluminium bodied version with a 100bhp TR3 engine which consis-

tently beat the TRs because it was considerably lighter. This Super Sports ended up winning the 2 litre GT class at Le Mans in 1962, to the incredulity of the French, who had turned the Le Mans entry down the year before on the grounds that it looked old-fashioned and therefore must be dangerous!

The 4/4 in time gained the ubiquitous Ford Cortina 1600cc engine and is still available in both two and four seater form. The open four seater sports car is a pre-war fashion that has otherwise disappeared; rear seat occupants are behind the rear axle and have a pretty bumpy ride.

Basically the same car, with the same simple 'Z' section chassis frame, the same wood-framed doors and floorboards and, until mid-1972, the same type of Moss gearbox mounted in the cockpit, separate from the engine, is the exciting Plus Eight. Depending on one's attitude,

this generated cries of glee or terror when it was introduced in 1968. It has the alloy $3\frac{1}{2}$ litre Rover V8 engine (derived from a Buick of the early 1960s) delivering 160bhp. The Plus 8 weighs only 17·7cwt. It will do 124mph and is faster to 90mph than a six cylinder Jaguar E-type. It is better mannered than one might expect—and can even give some specially prepared rally cars a run for their money on rough roads if the driver is skilful and brave enough—but it is not a car to be trifled with. It is tremendous fun in an old-fashioned manner. That is hardly surprising, and definitely the way traditional Morgan enthusiasts want it. At Morgan it is only the move towards conformity which goes slowly.

The Complicated World of International Racing

For the purpose of this book, we don't need a rigid definition of a sports car. But those who lay down the rules for motor sport at an international level, the *Commission Sportive Internationale* (CSI) of the *Fédération Internationale de l'Automobile* (FIA) do need one. They have to produce a very precise set of regulations for sports car racing in an attempt to retain some characteristics of everyday road cars. These rules are, not surprisingly, a constant source of argument. Because of its ever-changing style, sports car racing has never enjoyed the status and popular appeal of Grand Prix racing, despite the fact that over the years it has attracted a greater number of major manufacturers than the premier single-seater formula.

Sports car racing arose as a means of entering competition with cars which were basically as you can buy. But, of course, right from the start competitors could find ways of making their cars that little bit quicker – by modifying the engine, shedding some weight or discarding some unnecessary equipment. Allowed to continue uncontrolled, it does not take very long for this sort of approach to produce something very like a Grand Prix car, a machine constructed and intended solely for the purpose of racing. So from early days rules have been framed to try to keep sports cars that race somewhere close to sports cars that one can buy and drive on the road. The very first Tourist Trophy in 1905 required 'standard bodies' but also set a chassis weight limit. In their attempts to lighten their cars for more speed but keep within the regulations, some competitors made up engine covers and running boards from cardboard! In the 1920s and 1930s it was not unusual for sports car to be modified versions of Grand Prix cars and vice versa. Several Bugattis and the famous 2·3 litre Alfa Romeo – which shared both engine and basic chassis design with the equally celebrated Monza Grand Prix car – were good examples of this. The 4·5 litre Talbot-Lago that won the 1950 Le Mans 24 Hour Race was unashamedly a Grand Prix car of the type that the team

Sports car racing in America. Watkins Glen, New York State, first hosted races through the streets of the town in 1948. The annual 24 Hour race at Daytona, a round of the World Championship for Manufacturers, attracts mixed bags of sports cars. In this shot is a Chevrolet Corvette, an MGB, a Porsche prototype and a Porsche GT

Porsche have been represented in all forms of sports car competition for many years. The 911 has performed well in rallies (like the Swedish Rally, right), tough road races like the Targa Florio (above), and high-speed circuit events where it has won the GT category while out-and-out sports-racing Porsches achieved overall victory. The centre photograph shows a Porsche 917 gobbling up a 911 through the 150mph Stavelot Corner at Spa-Francorchamps in Belgium, the fastest road circuit in Europe. In 1971 a 917 set a new lap record at Spa of 162·1mph.

The psychedelic 'whale' (left) was a special super-aerodynamic version of the 917 designed for Le Mans; it finished second in the wet 1970 race. In 1971 the 24-hour race was won by the conventional short-tailed 5-litre 917 driven by Helmut Marko and Gijs van Lennep (above)

had been racing all that season, fitted with skimpy cycle-type wings and lights.

But however controversial and unpopular some of these 'special' sports cars might have been at the time, they mattered less than the changes which took place in sports car racing later in the 1950s and continued through the next 20 years. The difference was that those Bugattis and Alfa Romeos *were* directly related to cars that one could buy and use quite satisfactorily on the road. The Grand Prix cars with which they shared engines and chassis were two seaters anyway (although carrying a riding mechanic in Grand Prix racing ceased in 1924) and with only minor changes to satisfy law, a fully fledged racing car *could* be used for a run down to the shops. Even that Le Mans-winning Grand Prix Talbot could claim to have its origins back in a production sports car of 1936.

Sports car racing used to be different from Grands Prix because it was concerned with *endurance*, both in the length of the event and the tough nature of the course. For today's car, with many more years of refinement behind it, it can be argued that even a 24 hour race is no longer a very severe test. Most races are in any case a great deal shorter, all but two being run over 1 000 kilometres (625 miles). With only a very few exceptions circuits are billiards-table smooth. High levels of sophistication in engine and chassis development, and aerodynamics, combined to make the so-called 'sports prototype' of the late 1950s an out-and-out racing car, and a rather strange one at that. By 1960 you could forget any thoughts about driving most of them on the road, even to reach the races in which they were to compete. (It should be said that tightening-up of motoring laws in most countries also had a bearing on this.)

Through the years following the Second World War, sports car racing has run in phases. Racing car designers are experts at finding loopholes in regulations. Their job is to win races, to give their drivers equipment superior to their rivals. They are not, and must not be,

Le Mans 1951: a win for the C-type Jaguar in its first appearance. The special competition Jaguar, based on the XK120, was driven by Peter Whitehead and Peter Walker, both of whom are shown sitting in the car after the finish

influenced by what is known as 'the spirit of the regulations'. It is not good enough to make it known what sort of car is envisaged when writing a set of regulations; those rules have to be framed in such a way as to prevent anyone building anything but that sort of car. Of course, this is almost impossible.

The rules governing sports car racing have to be very artificial. Attempts to relate them to road cars, by requiring such things as high windscreen and windscreen wipers, hoods, full passenger seats and luggage space are looked upon as a hindrance by the designers because *racing* sports cars do not need them. A passenger seat is not necessary if there is never to be more than one person in the car, a trunk useless if there is no need to carry any luggage, and a high windscreen unnecessary in an open car when the driver has to wear a crash helmet and goggles anyway.

So what starts off as a category for fairly standard cars, gradually evolves more and more specialised prototypes, which in turn results in

the further relaxation of regulations until someone cries: 'Stop! This is getting silly – let's go back to production cars again.' The manufacturers, who are usually by then becoming embarrassed by the efforts and expense required to keep up with the tide of development, gratefully agree. There have been several attempts to 'normalise' sports/racing cars over the last 20 years, but none have met with lasting success. To be sure, there have been many genuine prototypes which later gave rise to new production cars – British manufacturers like Jaguar, MG and Triumph are among those who have tried and proved new ideas in this way – but this 'experimental' function of sports car racing would seem to be drawing to a close.

The most successful way of ensuring that the cars that race are related to the cars that we can buy is to reserve the events for models which are already in production, of which a certain minimum number have been made. Exactly what that number should be is questionable— and very important. If the figure is too high, small firms who produce genuinely suitable cars may not reach the production requirement and would therefore be unfairly excluded. If it is too low then a rich manufacturer can undertake to build the set number of cars for racing alone. Just that happened in 1969, as we shall see later.

Le Mans sets the style

Of all sports car races—indeed of all motor races—the Le Mans 24 Hour Race is the most famous. Traditionally a race for series production cars, it was this French classic which, perhaps unwittingly, started the trend towards prototypes when it resumed in 1949 after ten years absence. It was a time of austerity, when the motor industry and racing people had no lack of new ideas but few opportunities to carry them out. The Automobile Club de l'Ouest, the Le Mans organisers, decided to allow prototypes 'to assist the industry to a more rapid return to normal conditions'. The 1949 race was won by Luigi Chinetti and Lord Selsdon in a Ferrari 166—which was, in effect, a prototype, for the now so famous Italian manufacturer was only just beginning to build cars under his own name.

A year later, in the race won by the 4½ litre Talbot-Lago referred to earlier, three Jaguar XK120s appeared in the 24 Hours. These were privately entered, were well-placed early in the race, and scored 12th and 14th places—an unremarkable result in itself, but one which was to encourage the Jaguar management to build a special version of the XK120 in a bid to win the event in the following year. This was the start of seven glorious years for the Coventry firm, seven years that brought them five wins in the French classic and all the prestige and publicity that went with it.

The 1951 Le Mans car was called the XK120C, later to be universally referred to as the C-type. It had a tubular chassis frame, was lighter, more streamlined and handled and

Bird's eye view of the Jaguar D-type, introduced in 1954. The passenger's space in this early version was normally covered by a metal hatch when racing. Later cars had a tail fin and full width windscreen

stopped better than the XK120, while extensive modifications extracted 200bhp from the 3·4 litre twin overhead camshaft engine, 40bhp more than the standard car. Driven by Peter Walker and Peter Whitehead it won the 24 Hours, first time out, by a generous margin. During the following year Jaguar's racing programme included the Mille Miglia, the fast, gruelling and dangerous race which looped the

heart of Italy on public roads. Stirling Moss's C-type for this event had an important modification— Dunlop disc brakes. These were a fitment which were to give Jaguar a significant advantage in the years to follow and provide the most often quoted example of how motor racing —and in this case long-distance racing in particular—'improves the breed'. Tested and developed in racing, disc brakes will soon be universal on road cars, from the slowest saloon to the fastest sports models.

The C-type was succeeded by the D-type in 1954. More powerful and

The Jaguar XKSS was a roadgoing version of the D-type intended for the American market; few were built

more advanced in almost every respect, it was to become a classic. Its shape was startling, with the cockpit surrounded by a deep wraparound windscreen faired into a headrest which later sported an upright fin. It was the type of body that was to set the trend for sports prototypes. One could be excused for thinking that it had only one seat, for the perch for the mythical passenger demanded by the regulations was concealed by a metal hatch flush with the bodywork (this was not a new idea, for the Bugatti which won at Le Mans in 1939 used a similarly aerodynamic arrangement). The D-type, winner at Le Mans in 1955, 1956 and 1957, as well as of innumerable other races the world over, was a true prototype.

Many of the lessons learned from the racing programme found their way on to Jaguar road cars at the time. Jaguar even put a version of the D-type into production for a while. This was the XKSS, which was specifically aimed at the American market. It was somewhat detuned compared to the racing 'D' but still one of the fastest road cars available in the 1950s. Only 16 were

built before a fire at the factory caused extensive damage and the company decided not to proceed with the XKSS.

The Jaguar factory withdrew from competition at the end of 1956 but continued to give support to private teams running their cars. A 3 litre capacity limit was imposed on the World Sports Car Championship for 1958 and although some Jaguar engines were reduced in capacity to comply, by that time the D-type design was getting old and met with little success. That seemed to close the Jaguar racing story–at least in endurance racing–but then in 1960 there appeared at Le Mans a mysterious Jaguar entered by the great American enthusiast Briggs Cunningham. It had a family resemblance to the D-type but under the skin had a new aluminium engine and independent suspension all round (it was the first Jaguar to

One of Briggs Cunningham's entries in the 1952 Le Mans race was this C4RK coupé, seen here chased by Moss' droop-nose C-type Jaguar. The coupé retired, but an open Cunningham finished fourth

have independent rear suspension). It was widely referred to as the E-type, though never officially called that. Jaguar had reserved that designation for a new roadgoing production car to be announced a year later, with exactly similar rear suspension and the same sleek lines . . .

America's great 'trier'

Briggs Cunningham had played a significant part in the development of sports car racing in America, the land of oval track speedway racing, where it was virtually unknown before the Second World War. There had been some small-time events held on dirt roads in New York State during the 1930s and from this nucleus indirectly arose the beginnings of the Sports Car Club of America which, in 1948, organised the first race meetings in the streets of the little holiday town of Watkins Glen, in the picturesque Finger Lakes region of New York. The SCCA today has 105 regions and 18 000 members and organises 300 events per year, including the United States Grand Prix and the Six Hour endurance race which takes place annually at the fine permanent circuit on the outskirts of 'The Glen'. Cunningham was one of their early supporters with such cars as Ferraris and a home-constructed Buick-Mercedes Special, and he set his sights on racing in Europe–with American cars.

In 1950 Cunningham came to Le Mans with two Cadillacs–one a stock saloon and the other an open two-seater based on the same chassis but with an extraordinary angular two-seater body which became

known as 'Le Monstre'. They finished 10th and 11th. A year later Cunningham returned with two new sports/racing cars bearing his name. They had tubular chassis, De Dion rear suspension and big (5.4 litre) Chrysler V8 engines. One contested second place for a while but eventually finished 18th. This was the first of a series of sports/racing cars from Cunningham which took part in the French race regularly until 1955, when he gave up the huge expenditure of producing his own cars and took to entering the products of other firms. He failed to achieve his ambition of winning Le Mans but his cars were not disgraced – they finished fourth in 1952, third in 1953 and third in 1954.

The Cunningham's only major victory was a very appropriate one, for it was in the Sebring 12 Hours in 1953, the first event of the first edition of the World Sports Car Championship. Alec Ulmann first organised motor racing on this desolate Florida airfield in December 1950; the idea of a 12-hour endurance race was first carried out in 1952. Sebring remained on the sports car championship schedule thereafter, but the old runways and link roads which made up the circuit steadily deteriorated until in 1972 the track was pronounced unsuitable for modern racing. Like most airfield circuits, Sebring left a lot to be desired, but it did establish international links for American motor racing and contributed a great deal to the tremendous rise in popularity of European-style road racing on that side of the Atlantic.

Enter the silver arrows

In 1952, the year before the World Sports Car Championship was initiated, there had been a particularly significant new entrant into sports car racing. Mercedes-Benz, so dominant in racing in the late 1930s, were picking up the pieces after the devastation of the War, and by 1952 had built an exciting new sports car. Like many competition cars of that year it had closed coupé bodywork – a style that was to come and go in the years to follow, depending partly on the regulations in force but, more especially on the design fashions of

the day. Mercedes' 300SL had a powerful (175 bhp originally) engine of only three litres inclined at an angle to allow a low bonnet line in a multi-tubular chassis, the sides of which were so high that the body needed the famous lift-up 'gull-wing' doors to allow reasonable entrance and exit. The silver cars scored a 1-2 victory at Le Mans after the Talbot driven for 22½ of the 24 hours by Levegh had retired as

Mercedes-Benz entered sports car racing with the 300SLR in 1955. It was virtually a two-seater version of their streamlined W196 Grand Prix car with a 3-litre engine. Among its successes during the season was a fine win in the Mille Miglia by this car driven by Britain's Stirling Moss with Denis Jenkinson in the passenger seat

an indirect result of his exhaustion.

The 300SL was a true prototype, for Mercedes stopped racing the cars at the end of the 1952 season and just over a year later announced a development of it as a production car. At the same time, 1954, they had re-entered Grand Prix racing with such an advanced car (the

W196) and with the backing of a strong team and heavy investment that all other teams felt immediately poor and outmoded relations. For 1955 they contracted an even more powerful team (with Stirling Moss to back up 1954 World Champion Juan Manuel Fangio) and announced that in addition to Grand Prix racing they would take part in the races of the World Sports Car Championship with a new car not

dissimilar in appearance to the streamlined single seater formula 1 cars, called the 300SLR. This was to use a 3 litre version of the straight-eight fuel-injected 2.5 litre formula 1 engine.

Mercedes timed their entry into the series for the Mille Miglia at the end of April. The team practised over the roads that made up the course for this Italian classic for many weeks beforehand. Carrying a co-driver was optional; Fangio elected to go it alone, while Moss took with him Denis Jenkinson, the

Continental Correspondent to *Motor Sport* magazine, who during practice logged the route, the hazards and the speeds of the corners. The notes were transferred to a roll of paper carried in the cockpit and unravelled as the race went on. This was the forerunner of the 'pace notes' used by today's rally crews, and combined with Moss's virtuosity at the wheel allowed them to break the myth that 'he who leads at Rome will not win the race' and go on to set an all-time record of 97·9mph for the 992 miles. It was the second Mille Miglia victory for Mercedes (Caracciola had won it for them back in 1931) and the only time a British driver won this great event. The Mille Miglia ceased to be run after 1957, when De Portago's Ferrari had left the road killing both occupants of the car and eleven spectators.

Le Mans in 1955 promised to be something of a highspot in postwar sports car racing. To challenge Mercedes there were full teams from Jaguar, Ferrari, Aston Martin and Maserati, plus a powerful Lagonda and a new Cunningham. Castelotti's 4·4 litre Ferrari went into the lead at the start but he was soon caught by the battling Jaguar and Mercedes driven respectively by Mike Hawthorn and Juan Manuel Fangio. Lap after lap these two fought it out on the *Circuit de la Sarthe*, shattering the lap record and providing the sort of spectacle which is rarely seen in long-distance racing —two of the great champions of the sport in near-equal cars driving for the glory of two major manufacturers. In fact it was a question not so much of how fast the cars went as how well they stopped. The Jaguar D-type had the Dunlop disc brakes first tried on the Mille Miglia C-type three years before, while Mercedes augmented its inferior inboard drum brakes with a huge rear flap which could be raised by operating a lever in the cockpit to act as an 'air brake'. But the contest between the two was never proved, for when the race was no more than 2½ hours old there was the accident in which the Mercedes of Levegh plunged into a spectator enclosure killing 82 people and

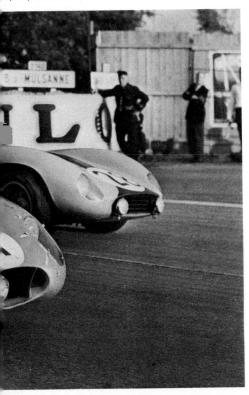

ove: An epic struggle at Le Mans, 1955
...en Mike Hawthorn (D-type Jaguar) and
...an-Manuel Fangio (Mercedes 300SLR)
...elled through the opening stage of the
...e, the Jaguar's disc brakes proving
...perior to the drums of the Mercedes which
...re augmented by a huge flap air brake (in
...eration here)

t: Lotus' aerodynamic little cars, like this
...rk XI, did well in the small capacity
...sses at Le Mans in the late 1950s

low: Maserati produced this coupé version
...the impressive 450S for Stirling Moss to
...ve at Le Mans in 1957. It is shown in
...mpany with a Ferrari Testa Rossa

injuring over 100 more. It was motor racing's darkest day. We shall never know if the Jaguar would have beaten Mercedes over the 24 hours, whether both cars would have lasted, or if the German car, which Fangio shared with Moss, would have held on to the two lap lead it had at midnight over the Hawthorn-Bueb D-type. At 1.45 a.m. the remaining Mercedes were withdrawn in respect for those who had died. Jaguar won – but it was a hollow victory.

The Le Mans disaster had widespread repercussions. Many races were cancelled, including two rounds of the sports car championship: the Nürburgring 1 000Kms and the PanAmerican road race, which had been part of the Championship since its inception. The next round after Le Mans became the Tourist Trophy at Dundrod, Northern Ireland, but that too was a victim of this fateful season, for three drivers lost their lives in accidents. Like the Targa Florio a few weeks later, Dundrod ended in a victory for Moss and these two victories at the end of the upset season gave Mercedes the Championship victory they had sought. The Stuttgart firm withdrew from racing, for they had achieved their objective. The 300SLR, unlike the 300SL coupé of three years before, was a pure racing car shaped to the regulations of sports car racing; in Mercedes production cars aggressiveness was reduced rather than increased over the succeeding years, as the emphasis was put on luxurious touring rather than stark speed.

Reaction to disaster
The Sports Car Championship reached a turning point at the end of 1955. The Le Mans circuit needed a number of safety modifications and the organisers of the 24-hour race decided unilaterally to restrict manufacturers' prototypes to a maximum capacity of 2·5 litres. Any car over that size had to be one of a production run of 100. The 24 Hours was therefore dropped from the 1955 Championship. It turned out to be a Ferrari year, although the result was in doubt until the last round, the newly admitted Swedish Grand Prix, when

five works Ferraris faced five works Maseratis and Ferrari took the first three places. For 1957 the CSI devised a new set of regulations under the heading of Appendix 'C'. It was a half-hearted attempt to bring the prototypes into line and adopted most of the previous year's Le Mans regulations, though the 2·5 litre capacity limit for prototypes was not included. The new rules required two doors, full-width windscreens and tops for open cars (these could be removed for racing and so didn't have to be practical).

In practice the new rules made precious little difference to the sort of cars produced for sports car racing. Maserati, who had managed to win two championship events with their 3-litre cars in 1956, relied mainly on the raucous 4·5 litre V8 450S – a big, brutish machine which again took two of the major races, though Ferrari won the Championship. Ferrari, who used a bewildering variety of cars and engines – not to mention drivers – during these years had the great virtue of nearly always being *there*, while other teams selected the events that best suited their cars (this particularly applied to Jaguar, who continued their success at Le Mans under the aegis of Ecurie Ecosse when the D-types were past winning elsewhere).

The 450S Maserati was the expensive straw that broke a financially weak team's back. Four works cars were wrecked in the last disastrous race of the 1957 season, in Venezuela, and then the CSI announced the 3-litre capacity limit for the 1958 Sports Car Championship.

That the CSI 3-litre rule did little to curtail the ever-increasing speeds was no real surprise (after all, the super-fast Mercedes of 1955 had been a 3-litre car). Under it, Aston Martin began to enjoy the success which had largely eluded them during many years of trying. They achieved second place at Le Mans in 1955, 1956 and 1958 with the DB3S and in 1956 the successor to this model, the DBR1, had appeared, initially in 2·5 litre form. In 1957, with the engine up to a full 3 litres, a DBR1 driven by Tony Brooks and Noel Cunningham Reid

The Ferrari 275GTB (right) was a fast close-coupled two-seater directly derived from racing practice; it was the first roadgoing Ferrari to have independent rear suspension. This design led to the 365 GTB/4 Daytona (below), which apart from being one of the fastest road cars in the world has also performed creditably at Le Mans

The Berlinetta Lusso of 1962 (right) is surely the most beautiful of all Ferraris

The Ferrari Dino (above) with a transversely-mounted V6 engine installed in a small, elegant body brought the possibility of Ferrari ownership to a wider market. Its introduction also meant that the output of the small factory at Maranello could be increased. Here all Ferraris are virtually hand-built (left)

had almost unexpectedly beaten the full might of the Italian teams in the 1000Km race at the Nürburgring. With a bigger programme and an impressive line-up of drivers in 1958, the success in the German race was repeated (by Moss and Brabham) while at the end of the season they finished 1-2-3 in the Tourist Trophy, held at the Goodwood circuit.

Encouraged, Aston Martin planned a strong effort for 1959 and patron David Brown declared their intention of winning at Le Mans. And this they achieved, notably by a combination of good preparation, careful team planning and fine pit work. Astons took first and second places and found themselves in with

Aston Martin won Le Mans in 1959 after years of trying. The car was a 3-litre DBR1/300 driven by Roy Salvadori and Carroll Shelby. A similar machine driven by Trintignant and Frère finished second

a chance of winning the Championship. They had already won the Nürburgring race (Moss again, this time with Jack Fairman), and there was just one race left, the Tourist Trophy. This was full of excitement as the leading Moss/Salvadori Aston Martin caught fire in the pits when refuelling and was burnt out. Moss took over the second team car of Carroll Shelby and Jack Fairman

A dramatic fire in the pits at Goodwood during the 1959 Tourist Trophy race wrecked one of the Aston Martin team cars, but they went on to win the race and seal the Manufacturers' Championship

and started after the leaders. In another display of driving brilliance, Moss put the Aston into the lead only an hour after all had seemed lost in the pits. Aston Martin won the race and became the only team using all-British equipment to win the world title.

Aston Martin, like Jaguar, believed in racing as a test-bed for their road cars. Brown wanted a class for cars closer to those you could buy and after their Championship win withdrew from racing subjected to what he considered were unrealistic regulations. Enzo Ferrari had expressed a similar view. The rules were changed for 1960, but not in the way these key gentlemen had hoped. Instead of adopting a production requirement and insisting on proper Grand Touring cars there and then, the CSI introduced a set of complicated regulations requiring high windscreens, a set amount of luggage space and several other items which they hoped would require the use of a GT-type car. In most cases it didn't, for manufacturers merely complained, and then adapted existing designs to the new rules with disastrous aesthetic results and severe visibility handicaps for the drivers.

This gave rise to some extraordinary freaks. Maserati had returned in a very limited way with a 2 litre sports car, the Tipo 60. With a very complicated chassis made of a multitude of tiny tubes, this car was quickly dubbed the 'Birdcage'. It was an ugly car even when it was introduced; fitted with a regulation high screen as it was when the engine size was increased to 2·9 litres for the 1960 T61, it became almost indescribably so. For Le Mans a long streamlined tail was fitted to one car, plus a huge windscreen which extended forward to the nose of the car and succeeded in making it look even more ridiculous. The Maserati people enjoyed the joke, particularly since the regulation windscreen wiper operated over an area above the driver's feet! It was legal and it worked, for Masten Gregory showed that it was the fastest car on the circuit in the opening stages of the race.

The mid-engine revolution

A feature of the later 1950s was the rise to prominence of Porsche. The German firm had been involved in sports car racing since 1951 and although, like others, their cars became some distance removed from their bread-and-butter production counterparts, they resisted the temptation to move out of the small capacity class where their sales were. Nonetheless, they had won the Targa Florio outright in 1956. (The Targa, now the last of the great road races to remain on the motoring calendar, uses the normal roads of the rugged Sicilian countryside and is well suited to a small, nimble car). By 1958, still with only 1·6 litres, they were able to cause some embarrassment to the larger Ferraris and Aston Martins on faster and more conventional circuits, especially where they had drivers of the quality of Moss and Jean Behra. They took the Targa Florio again in 1959, starting a run of consistent success in this event, and had stood to win the Tourist Trophy that year had Moss and Aston Martin not recovered so well from their pit fire. Sebring was added to their score of outright wins in 1960.

In the early 1950s Porsche seemed to be way out of step with the mainstream of sports car design. Their cars had engines at the back—later in the middle—and those engines were air-cooled. The latter was not a characteristic that was to be widely emulated (although Porsche continue with air cooling to this day) but not long after Cooper had started the revolution in Formula 1 with their lightweight mid-engined cars, racing sports cars began to follow suit. In February 1961 Ferrari announced his new prototypes. One was an updated version of the V12 'Testa Rossa', which had served the team so well since the beginning of the 3-litre limit and the other, similarly 'nostril' nosed and high-tailed, was the Tipo 246 with a 2·5 litre V6 Dino engine mounted amidships. At a casual glance the two cars were not easy to distinguish but the die was cast, for by the end of the 1962 season the front-engined Ferrari had scored its last great victory, at Le Mans in the hands of that tre-

Maserati's long screen on the T61 at Le Mans in 1960 met the letter, if not the spirit of the regulations, which attempted to move prototypes nearer to production cars. It is shown in company with one of the Camoradi Corvettes

mendous long-distance partnership of Phil Hill and Olivier Gendebien. At the same time as the Dino Ferrari was being developed Maserati were working on a mid-engined version of the 'Birdcage' with a 3-litre V12 engine.

This trend towards mid-engines only made the argument for a reversal to more standard cars stronger and in 1962 the sports car champion-

Phil Hill signals oil on the track at Le Mans in 1962. His win with the 4-litre Ferrari Testa Rossa variant was his third in the 24 Hours, in each case partnered by Olivier Gendebien

ship as such was abandoned, the CSI instituting instead a contest for series production GT cars. But the four 'classics'—Sebring, the Targa Florio, the Nürburgring 1 000 Kilometres and Le Mans—continued to be run for prototypes. The Le Mans organizers even lifted the 3-litre limit, thus allowing in new 4-litre cars from Aston Martin and Maserati, both big front engined coupés.

The GT championship and another which encompassed the four prototype races, were run at the same time. It was a very confusing period, in which Ferraris won nearly everything in both categories when they fielded serious entries, but because they didn't always contest

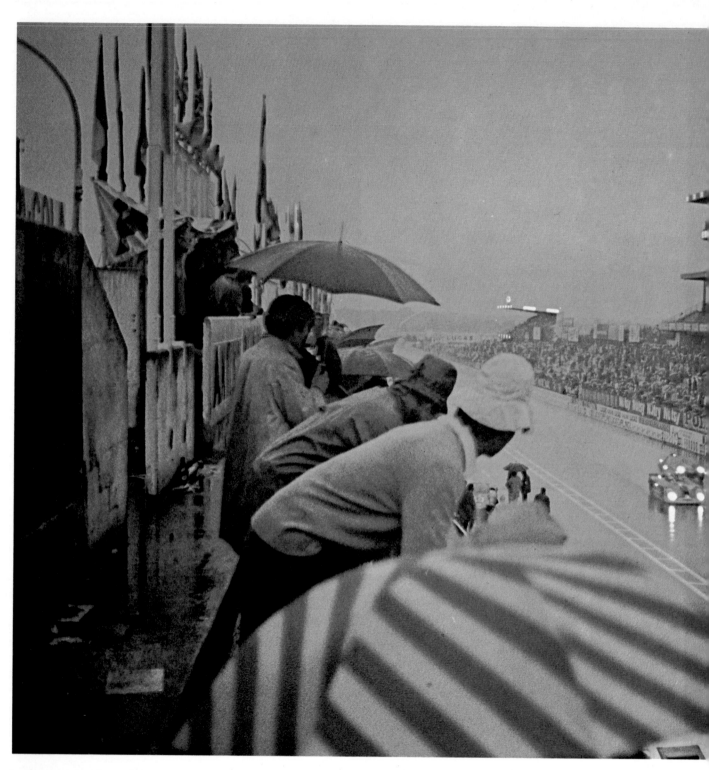

both groups they did not win the championships each year. The important point about these muddled times was that the prototype as a breed for its own sake was not killed, rather new and even more extraordinary sports/racing cars were actually developed. By 1967 there was a bigger prototype championship which included virtually all of the important sports car races.

An injection of dollars
In 1964 Ford of America entered the

scene with the GT40. They were not interested in championships or classes; their object, like that of so many manufacturers before them, was to win at Le Mans. To this end Ford tried to buy out Ferrari, and when this failed found themselves competing head on with the Maranello team, using advanced mid-engined coupés designed by Eric Broadley of Lola Cars in collaboration with Ford's Roy Lunn. Ford were already successfully involved in the GT category with

Carroll Shelby's AC Cobras when the GT40 first appeared at the Nürburgring in 1964.

The sleek new Ford failed to finish a race that year, though it led briefly at Le Mans. Ferrari were still winning, but Ford came back with a modified car the next year, substituting the Cobra-type 4·7 litre V8 engine from their production saloon range for the 4·2 litre Indianapolis unit first employed. They won the opening race of the 1965 season at Daytona. A new version of the car,

The 250LM was an early attempt by Ferrari to build a production mid-engined racing coupé. The CSI refused to recognise it as a GT car. The 250LM had a 3·3 litre engine

By this time the production requirement to qualify as a GT car had been reduced from 100 to 50 examples, and by offering some detuned GT40s for sale as road cars as well as making racing versions available to private owners, the GT40 could meet that bill. It was all getting out of hand – the fastest, most powerful and most expensive prototypes ever seen were winning the races, and the 'production sports/GT' category for more normal cars was now to include its only slightly less sophisticated brother. Something had to be done, and the CSI reacted by reintroducing the World Sports Car Manufacturers' Championship in 1968 and putting capacity limits on both 'Sports Cars' (known as Group 4) and prototypes (Group 6). Thus, a sports car of a maximum engine capacity of 5 litres which was one of a minimum production run of 50 was ranged against a 3-litre prototype. The 7-litre Fords were outlawed, but that didn't matter a lot as the American company withdrew anyway, having done what they set out to do, and the interesting Chevrolet-powered Chaparral, with its automatic transmission and overhead aerofoil 'wing' also became ineligible.

The 1968 rules meant, in effect, a

called the Mk II and fitted with the huge 485bhp 7-litre Ford Galaxie engine, was hurriedly prepared in time for Le Mans, but once again they all retired. With the investment being mounted Ford were not likely to suffer this record of non-achievement for long and in 1966 there were no mistakes, the Mk IIs taking the first three places in the 24 Hours, following up earlier wins in American races. In 1967 a more advanced version of the 7-litre Ford, the Mk 4, took Le Mans again.

Above: Darkness descends on Le Mans. The view from the top of the pits looking towards the main grandstand and the press box. It's eight o'clock, raining, and there are twenty damp hours to go

Right: In 1963 and 1965 a joint project by Rover and BRM produced gas turbine powered sports prototypes for the Le Mans 24 Hours. In 1963 the car ran outside the main race and carried the numbers '00'; it covered 4172km and qualified for a special prize. Two years later this elegant coupé version competed as a normal entry and, driven by Graham Hill and Jackie Stewart, finished tenth overall despite overheating troubles. More recently – in 1968 – an American car built by the Howmet Corporation has raced in sports car championship races using a gas turbine helicopter engine

straight fight between the Group 4 Ford GT40s (the most effective of which were the cars raced in the colours of the Gulf Oil Corporation by John Wyer, who ran the company responsible for the production and maintenance of GT40s), and the works Porsches. Ferrari was annoyed at the 3-litre prototype limit and did not race officially all year. Porsche won the championship and in doing so their cars 'grew up', with an increase in capacity from the 2·2 litres of the 907 model to a full 3 litres for the eight-cylinder engine of the 908. With the 908, the German company clearly took the 1969 championship.

For 1969 two things happened. The Group 6 rules were relaxed again to allow cut-down windscreens and a near reversion to the bodywork situation of the mid-1950s; and the production requirement for Group 4 was reduced from 50 to 25 cars per annum. The latter was perhaps intended to make it easier for some manufacturers to qualify with existing cars, but it had another far-reaching effect. It was a mistake.

How much of a mistake became clear at the 1969 Geneva Motor Show, when Porsche showed the 917 coupé, a big brute of a car, low

slung with a tiny closed cockpit. Its vastly long finned tail section enclosed a phenomenal 4·5 litre flat-12 engine producing, it was claimed, over 520bhp. Furthermore, they had pledged to build 25 of them to meet the 'sports car' regulations. They were priced at £14000, much less than they actually cost to build, but Porsche's budgeting was such that they did not really need to sell any; 25 cars could be used in their own racing effort over a couple of seasons. So here was a 'sports car' which was so far removed from the realities of normal use that it could not, by any stretch of the imagination, be driven safely on the road. Porsche had driven a 240mph bolt

Top: Ford were involved in both the AC Cobra (centre) and the Ford GT40 (right) racing programmes in 1964. This is the GT40's first race, at the Nürburgring

Above: By 1967 the GT40 had developed into the 7-litre Mark IV, which won Le Mans, driven by Dan Gurney and A. J. Foyt

through a loophole in the regulations.

Ferrari, who returned to the scene in 1969 with a 3-litre, felt obliged to follow suit and subsequently announced that in 1970 they too would build 25 Group 4 cars using a 5-litre V12 engine and called the 512. The scene was set for a confrontation between these Thoroughly Modern Monsters in the 1970 season.

Porsche withdrew their factory

Top: In 1967 Chaparral brought the overhead 'wing' to sports car racing. The Chaparral 2F won the BOAC 500 at Brands Hatch (here leading Stewart's Ferrari)

Above: The Ford of Britain 3-litre prototype built in 1968 was fast but never fully developed. It had a Formula 1 Cosworth V8

team at the end of 1969 and entrusted the 917s to John Wyer's team (who had beaten them earlier that year with an old GT40 in the closest-ever Le Mans finish), and to their Austrian subsidiary. The German cars won all the races but Sebring. The 917s were in any case more powerful and more sophisticated than the Ferrari, especially after a full 5-litre engine had been introduced at mid-season. They achieved their ultimate ambition when the Porsche Salzburg car driven by Richard Attwood and Hans Herrmann won a very wet Le Mans 24 Hour Race.

Once again the situation had become ludicrous. The advent of these 'super Group 4s' had meant that the 3-litre prototypes did not stand a chance except on twisty circuits like the Targa Florio and the Nürburgring – and for those Porsche came up with some ultra-light 3-litre 908 'specials'. It was decided that from 1972 the sports and prototype categories would be combined into one class with no production requirement, but new weight limits and a capacity restriction of 3 litres, which coincidentally was the same as the limit in operation for formula 1 Grand Prix racing. Porsche complained and threatened withdrawal, while Ferrari lost interest in the soon to be obsolete 512 and pressed on with the development of the formula 1-based 312P. Porsche won the 1971 Championship, with Alfa Romeo, who had returned to sports car racing back in 1967 with a 2 litre car called the T33, scoring three satisfying victories with their T33/3 3-litre car which had been overshadowed by the combined efforts of Porsche and Ferrari the year before.

However ill-conceived these ultra-powerful cars may have been, they provided a fine spectacle in days when racing cars are often rightly accused of appearing to corner 'on rails'. The 3-litre category which took their place palled by comparison. The cars were tiny, highly effective and almost as fast as the formula 1 cars, with which in most cases, they shared engines. Ferrari had

their most successful sports car season ever in 1972, winning 10 out of the 11 Championship races; the odd one out was Le Mans which they did not enter and which was won in equally convincing style by the French Matra team.

Two seater racing cars

With such a large investment in the 5-litre car and no suitable 'Grand Prix' engine, Porsche did withdraw and went CanAm racing instead. CanAm – the Canadian American Challenge Cup – started in 1966 as a series for cars with two seater all-enveloping bodies and the minimum of other restrictions. These cars,

Dominant cars. Porsche' second Le Mans victory was scored by this Martini Racing Team 917 driven by Helmut Marko and Gijs van Lennep in 1971

Right: The Ferrari 312P was unbeatable in 1972 when these cars won 10 out of 11 championship rounds

which by 1971 were using American V8 engines as large as 8·3 litres, became the fastest and most powerful competition cars in the world. They are in no sense sports cars and even the CSI define them as 'two seater racing cars', but they are only one step removed from the smaller sports prototypes and show how this category would have developed had it been left completely uncontrolled.

That so many manufacturers and teams were prepared to build and race such highly specialised and expensive machines is evidence of the huge prize funds that CanAm presented. But even here unlimited developments were checked. Jim Hall's Chaparral 2J—the latest in a series of cars which had always bristled with exciting innovations— appeared in 1970 with what was known as a 'ground effect' system. In essence, this was a little two-stroke engine mounted in the back of the car which drove a fan and literally sucked the air out from beneath it, giving the car greater adhesion to the road. It ran only a few races before lobbying from other teams caused it to be banned. Porsche became similarly unpopular, especially with the McLaren team who had won the CanAm series five years in a row with their immaculate Chevrolet-powered cars, when they introduced exhaust-driven turbochargers to obtain over 900bhp from their, by CanAm standards, 'little' 5-litre engines. They won the championship in 1972.

But, interesting as these developments may be, they do not belong to a discussion about the evolution of the sports car. Nor really does the ultra-specialised 3-litre prototype. By 1972 it had lost all vestiges of road equipment: the wide cockpit, the proper windscreen, the spare wheel, even the lights in events where they were not needed. It had become a Grand Prix racing car with a wider chassis and a skimpy shell of glass fibre covering the wheels.

It was no wonder then the enthusiasts' biggest cheer at Le Mans was for the modified Ford Capris which finished 10th and 11th. Critics of the motor racing scene were calling for a return to production GT and touring cars. Excuse me, but this is where we came in . . .

CanAm racing. The Chaparral 2J (top) had an ingenious system of fans and a flexible plastic 'skirt' to create suction under the car; it was banned. Porsche concentrated on CanAm in 1972 and with the aid of a turbocharged 900bhp engine, George Follmer (centre) won the championship, breaking a five year run of success for the McLaren team. Their 1972 M20 was a natural development of earlier McLarens. Denny Hulme took the author for a ride in the M20 at Goodwood (right)

The Last of the Great Road Racers

0–100mph in 8·8 seconds. Professional road testers reckon that a time like that for a zero-to-*sixty* miles per hour acceleration run is the mark of a fast car. Look at it this way: a Ferrari Daytona with 4·4 litres of V12 power, achieves 0–100 in around 12·5 seconds; at the time (1971) it was the fastest car that *Autocar* magazine had ever tested. But 8·8 seconds–*what* was that? It was a racing car, of course–a rather

Above: The Lola GT as it first appeared at the 1963 Racing Car Show. It was raced only occasionally

Right: Key men in the GT40's development. John Wyer (left), Eric Broadley (centre) and Ford's Roy Lunn (right), with the first car soon after completion

significant one, a Le Mans winner: John Wyer's 1969 Ford GT40.

The GT40 in its various forms won the Le Mans 24 Hour Race three times, while a more highly developed machine along the same lines–the Mk 4–added another win to that impressive score. Its origins are back in a neat little coupé called simply the Lola GT which was the star of the London Racing Car Show in 1963. By the standards of the time it was amazing–small, ultra-low and light in weight, powered by a

4·2 litre Ford V8 engine in the midships position that had become standard fashion for Grand Prix cars a couple of years before. The chassis was a monocoque construction, fabricated from aluminium alloy sheet, aircraft style. With its great power and light weight it promised to be capable of 200mph.

The giant Ford Motor Company of the United States wanted to build just such a car for their all-out attack

in international sports car racing. The Lola was the work of a quiet engineer called Eric Broadley who worked from a small establishment in Bromley, Kent. Looking back, perhaps the most significant thing about Broadley's design–which was

very advanced in all sorts of ways– was his decision to use a big American V8 engine, instead of one of the more sophisticated European racing power units. It was in later years to lead a new breed of cars which formed the backbone of the CanAm series.

Lola lacked the resources to develop their new car properly and it raced only a few times in 1963, latterly with a Chevrolet engine.

That was an interesting twist in view of what was to happen, for Broadley was offered a year's contract by Ford to design and build a new car along the same lines but to be called the Ford GT; the suffix '40' merely referred to the height of

The Mark I roadgoing GT40 is an exciting machine—it handles like the racing car that it is, has a sparkling performance from even a mildly tuned Ford V8 engine. The disadvantages of noise, poor insulation and ventilation, and lack of luggage space were largely improved for the Mark III

By 1968 the GT40, privately operated by John Wyer's Gulf-backed team among others, was competing against lighter and more nimble 3-litre Porsches, but it did score a significant victory in the BOAC 500 at Brands Hatch driven by Jacky Ickx and Brian Redman (opposite), as well as going on to win Le Mans

the car. The GT40 appeared in public for the first time at the Le Mans test weekend in April, 1964 and both examples crashed. Its first race was in the Nürburgring 1000 Kilometres a month later. The car failed to finish a single race in that first season, mainly because of transmission failures, but there was no doubt that it was fast. The Le Mans cars were even quicker the following year, having the 7-litre Ford Galaxie engine in a revised chassis known as the Mark II. It was these cars that in 1966 scored the first-ever win by an American car at Le Mans.

A key person in the early development of the project was John Wyer. He had worked with Aston Martin and ran their racing team with an icy efficiency in the years leading up

to that firm's championship win in 1959. He was to head the Ford team in that first, unsuccessful year on the sports car circuits and later to run the privately-sponsored GT40s that won at Le Mans in 1968 and 1969. Furthermore, he was in charge of the operation in England called Ford Advanced Vehicles Ltd, who were to manufacture GT40s for sale for racing and road use.

The idea of a roadgoing version of the Le Mans winner was hatched quite early in the GT40 story. It was a big publicity catcher. It allowed the car to qualify as a GT rather than a racing prototype. The early road versions did not differ a great deal from the racers. A little more interior trim, a few more instruments, carburettor air cleaner and silencers

on the exhausts, a couple more mirrors and lights, and off you went, turning the nearest motorway into your private Mulsanne Straight. Of course, the engines were not as powerful as those of the works machines – their fairly standard 4·7 litre Ford Fairlane V8 engine gave about 325bhp – and would not produce the sort of performance figures which opened this chapter. The acceleration was about the same as the Ferrari Daytona we discussed then, with a maximum speed of around 160mph. The first four gears of the five-speed ZF gearbox gave 61, 90, 128 and 140mph.

Unlike smaller European engines designed specifically for racing, the big Ford is not a temperamental engine and will tick-over without

Above: Engine room of the J. W. Engineering GT40 that won Le Mans in 1969; note the doors with wide roof cut-outs for easy access and the thick tank-containing sills

Left: This open car was another variant of the GT40, which appeared in Le Mans trials

need for the throttle blipping so enjoyed by racing enthusiasts. Fifth gear – top – can be used comfortably below 30mph. Installed in a low closed car, however, with the carburettor gulping fuel at around 12mpg adjacent to one's left ear (and separated from it only by a glass panel) it is infernally noisy.

Despite softer springing and slightly altered suspension, the handling and roadholding set standards unmatched by virtually any-thing else on the road, then or now. The precise high-geared steering and the brakes were straight from the racer and worked very, very well.

In performance, then, the road-going Mark I GT40 had few peers. But it was criticised, partly because of the poor quality of the interior equipment, which did not match up to that of other exotic cars in the £6 000-plus class, and also because many of those who drove it felt that a car which was no higher than the waist-line of a family saloon forced its driver and passenger to recline almost to the point of lying down, poured water on them when they opened the door in the rain, and failed to provide any more than a couple of overheated cubby holes for luggage, just was not a practical proposition for road use.

The shape, size and style of the GT40 has since been widely emu-lated by the designers of road cars and has set the trend for the more advanced sports cars of the 1970s. Some of the disadvantages with such a layout are common to them all, but more specific complaints about the GT40 like the noise, poor ventila-tion and difficulties of getting in and out have been solved by those that followed.

Ford Advanced Vehicles went some way towards this themselves with the Mark III, a special and more powerful version which re-placed the Mark I road car in 1967. Equipped with bumpers and a re-vised lighting system to meet tight-ening American regulations, it also had a lot more sound deadening

Above: Objective achieved—Chris Amon, Bruce McLaren and the team after Ford's first Le Mans win, in 1966 with the Mk II

Right: The Ickx-Redman J.W.A. GT40 at Daytona,1968

Bottom: The most civilised GT40—the Mk III

material and a new interior layout. The gear lever was moved from its racing position on the right hand side to the centre, but while this made entry over the wide tank-containing door sills a little easier (previously it was easier to end up with the gear lever up a trouser leg than a right foot in the pedal well), it had an adverse effect on what was a superb gearchange. Only a handful of Mark IIIs were built before production of the GT40 finally ceased in 1969.

Less than a hundred examples, including racing and road cars, were made during the five years. 0–100 in 8·8 seconds ? Sports/racing cars have subsequently gone much quicker than that, with a highspot at the 5-litre Porsche 917 which reached 235mph at Le Mans in 1971. But neither that nor its successors could be remotely suitable for road use. There are those who maintain that a true sports car is just as at home on the track as it is on the road. If that is so, the Ford GT40 could be the last dual-purpose road and track sports car.

73

Exotic, Experimental, Expensive

In this age of mass-production there will always be those who will value a hand-built product, one produced with loving care in exclusively small numbers. There will also be those who can afford, and will be prepared to pay for, a motor car which is 'different', which for reasons of style, luxury, performance or engineering perfection is set apart from the usual run of road transport. Such cars are usually of a sporting nature. It is true that the most expensive catalogued cars today are the Rolls-Royce and Mercedes limousines, but these are designed to provide the height of motoring luxury at the rear seat—and to be driven by a hired chauffeur.

However good they are, enjoyment of driving is not the primary consideration. In terms of car development they are a luxurious backwater, and do not concern us.

Just as the latest Paris Collection sets the trends for next year's clothes in the High Street *boutique*, so can the exotic cars of today provide a glimpse of the motoring future. 'Dream cars' often become reality in the rarified atmosphere of the coachwork sections of the world's motor shows, and in particular at Turin, traditionally the most important automobile showplace. All but a very few of the masters of body design operate in Italy and it is that country where most of the specialist

manufacturers who adopt their more radical ideas are to be found. For most of them *production* is a relative term, for at £10 000 each, making a few cars a year can be satisfactory business. Ferrari and Lamborghini sell fewer than 500 V12 cars each per year, but they are in the big league compared to most of their competitors.

Their technique, and that of the coachbuilders, is to produce a design, build a prototype, exhibit it and test reaction. If there is a

The Boxer BB is the first 'full-size' mid-engined road car from Ferrari. It has a 4·4 litre flat-12 engine developing 360bhp and a five-speed gearbox. Though intended for high-speed touring it will make a competitive GT racing car

The Alfa Romeo Montreal (top) is a conventional front-engined car of some sophistication. It uses a 2·6 litre V8 engine directly derived from that of the T33 sports prototype.

The Maserati Bora (centre) is the first mid-engined road car from this Modenese manufacturer. Its appearance is heavy, but the design is practical in that the Bora has more luggage space than is usual for this type of car. A 4·7 litre V8 engine ensures sparkling performance

Designed by Bertone as a 'racer' type rally car for high-speed tarmac events, the Lancia Stratos (left) has a Ferrari Dino engine mounted amidships

demand they can subsequently build replicas.

We have already discussed how the Lamborghini Miura set the trend for future road sports cars along a mid-engined course. The Miura has gone, replaced by the Countach, an even more rakish looking mid-engined design (with power unit running longitudinally, not transversely) which had been shown as a prototype many months earlier. Ferruccio Lamborghini was, and is, a tractor manufacturer, based near Bologna. The story goes that he owned a Ferrari and wished to complain about its poor performance to Enzo Ferrari in person. An audience was not granted and Lamborghini was so incensed that he vowed to build GT cars of his own which would be better than Ferraris. The legend may not be true—but the objective certainly was. In 1963 Automobili Lamborghini started by building a $3\frac{1}{2}$ litre V12 engine, installed it in an adequate chassis, but then clothed the whole with a two-seater body which was too cluttered in design to be pretty or even particularly startling. The latter was not a mistake that they were to repeat, for the next all-new Lamborghini was the first to be named after a type of fighting bull—the Miura. This was to put them firmly on the super-car map and it

Left: Lamborghini started building front-engined GT cars in 1963 with similar two seater and 'two-plus two' bodies—this one is a 400 GT 2+2. The beautiful Espada (below) —a true four seater—uses the same V12 engine and was developed from the Marzal show car

was quickly followed by another show car, which providing it gained the same ready acceptance would also become a production model. It was also mid-engined, though with a 2 litre engine and *four* passable seats, as well as glass doors and sides giving goldfish-bowl visibility (and exposure). This was the futuristic Marzal first shown at Geneva in 1967. The idea did not quite catch on (potential buyers did not like the small engine or the glass gull-wing doors) so the same basic shape was cleverly scaled-up, the 4 litre V12 engine installed in the front, and the four seater Lamborghini became the Espada, a truly impressive look-ing car which was to be one of the hallmarks of the 'jet-set' rich.

In a few short years Lamborghini became a manufacturer of some of the world's most exciting cars. That he did so without the glamorous associations of a racing background is a tribute to the bold engineering and dramatic Bertone-designed bodies of his cars. Certainly Ferrari lost quite a lot of potential business as a result. Ferrari has never gone in for styling extravagances to draw attention to his road cars and these are inclined to be conservative in their mechanical design. There have been many outstanding special bodies on Ferrari chassis, to be sure, but more to satisfy the whim of the designer or an individual customer than the Ferrari factory. This con-servatism meant that it was a long time before Ferrari road cars had really adequate brakes, even longer before they had independent rear

The 'wedge' theme has been prevalent in design exercises of recent years. Top left is the Lotus Espirit built on a Lotus Europa chassis by Ital-Design and shown at the 1972 Turin Show. The Carabo (left) was perhaps the clearest and most celebrated example of the wedge style. Though scarcely practical as it stands, some of the ideas it exhibited were good. The windows are made from a 'one way' Sundym glass. The Carabo, like several other 'dream car' projects is based on an Alfa Romeo racing chassis. Bertone's Lamborghini Countach (above), is the successor to the Miura and billed as the fastest production car in the world. With a 5-litre V12 engine its maximum speed is said to be close to 200mph

suspension, and only in 1973 did a full-size mid-engined road Ferrari get into production. Even so, in the author's view the Maranello *marque* has presented at least four road models which set new visual standards, each of which represented the near-ultimate car of its era.

The oldest of these and arguably the most beautiful of all was the Berlinetta Lusso, introduced in 1962. A masterpiece by Pininfarina, it synthesised the best features of the short-wheelbase 250GT which was raced very successfully in the early 1960s and the GTO which followed it. The Lusso had a milder version of the famous and marvellous-sounding V12 engine than the

Opposite: Two classic Ferraris—the racing GT064 (above) and the 250GT short-wheelbase Berlinetta (below). The Berlinetta shown is Rob Walker's car driven at Goodwood by Stirling Moss. This car gave rise to the Lusso, shown on page 58, while the GTO indirectly resulted in the 275GTB

Right: The De Tomaso Pantera is an attractive mid-engined two seater using an American Ford V8 engine. It succeeded the controversial Mangusta which looked splendid but did not handle as well. Ford's investment in the De Tomaso company resulted in the Pantera being adopted as part of the Lincoln-Mercury line in the United States

racing GTO, producing 250bhp. The final (1964) version of the GTO (the 'O' stood for *Omologato*; meaning it complied with, in this case, GT rules) stood out as an extremely elegant but functional racing GT with a low, small cockpit set well back, a steeply-raked windscreen and an aerodynamic tail treatment reminiscent of the otherwise much less attractive mid-engined 250LM racer.

The other two favourites were developments of the 275 GTB. This was the first production Ferrari to have independent rear suspension and with it came the location of the gearbox at the rear in unit with the differential. Its Pininfarina-designed body had an aggressive get-up-and-go look which was very appropriate to a 160mph car. In 1966 it became the 275GTB/4 when the 300bhp four overhead camshaft version of the 3·3 litre V12 was fitted. A super-streamlined body, also designed by Pininfarina, and a

320bhp 4·4 litre version of the four-cam V12, turned the 275GTB into the Daytona (also known as the 365GTB/4). It was Ferrari's answer to the Miura, which had laid claim to being the World's fastest road car. Such claims are controversial, partly because these low-production specialised cars vary quite a lot from one to another, but when *Autocar* tested it in 1971 the Daytona did manage 174mph, which was 2mph quicker than the Miura. One thing most testers did agree was that the Daytona represented just about the ultimate in practical roadgoing sports cars. There will doubtless be better cars in the future but this Ferrari could remain at the pinnacle

of *front-engined* two seaters.

Ferrari is not to be rushed. Lamborghini went mid-engined, others followed, but it needed the Dean of the exotic car school—the *Commendatore* from Maranello—to give the concept his seal of approval. Apart from the little Dino, that approval was implied in the Pininfarina Berlinetta Boxer which first appeared at Turin in 1971. An angular, no-frills body clothed a 360bhp 4·4 litre 12-cylinder engine built in horizontally-opposed 'boxer' fashion like the Ferrari formula 1 and prototype cars. This fabulous machine is said to be capable of 190mph.

Ferrari's great opponents on the track for many years—Maserati—had already followed the mid-engined fashion. After a few successful years with the 4·7 litre V8 engined Ghibli and the 2+2 Indy, they built a rather heavy-looking

170mph mid-engined device called the Bora.

By 1971, however, Ferrari and Maserati had an opponent in this market, selling cars of similar concept and not much less performance at a considerably lower price. This was De Tomaso. Alessandro De Tomaso had gained a reputation as an automobile inventor; he built cars, engines, single-seater racing cars, sports-prototypes—all sorts of projects which were proudly exhibited, and then never seen again. But with the beautiful mid-engined Mangusta, powered by an American Ford V8 engine, his business took a more serious turn. He bought out the Ghia and Vignale coach-build-ing firms and in due course the giant Ford Motor Company bought a controlling interest in his organisation. The much-criticised Mangusta gave way to the Pantera, another beautiful styling job, which was adopted by Ford as the most expensive car in their Lincoln-Mercury line. In truth, the De Tomaso doesn't begin to match the all-round standards of, say, a Ferrari, but achieves much of the *charisma* of such cars at a significantly lower price by the old trick of using a big, cheap American engine instead of a multi-camshaft Italian thorough-bred.

The Pantera was nearer in price to the Ferrari Dino than the Daytona and its more commodious stable-mates. Suddenly a new market had appeared in lower-priced (if still very expensive) exotica —in Britain, around the £6000 mark.

Ferrari had the transverse mid-engined Dino, Maserati made a cheaper (and neater) version of the Bora called the Merak with a 3-litre V6 engine and Lamborghini went into production with the futuristic Urraco with a transverse-mounted 2·5 litre V8 and some token rear seats. These lined up against the conventional front-engined Alfa Romeo Montreal (with a detuned racing V8 engine), the very advanced Citroen SM (with Maserati power), the more expensive of the BMW and Fiat GT coupés, and the top end of the Porsche 911 range. It was a bewildering choice—if one had the money!

Dreams that can come true

It is this slightly smaller size of car which has been represented by many of the more interesting 'dream car' styling exercises of recent years. Alfa Romeo's 2 litre T33 sports/racing car was never a tremendous success on the race track but its unusual tubular chassis has been in great demand as the basis for mid-engined styling projects. (Alfa did, in fact, build some chassis for their own road-equipped T33 *stradale* of which about twenty were sold in 1968 and 1969). Probably the most significant design so equipped was Bertone's Carabo, a thoroughly impractical fluorescent green armadillo-like coupé which nonetheless has set a style for future sports and GT cars. The mid-engined location allows the line of the steeply raked windscreen to continue to the flat spade-like nose of the car, while the tail is cut-off for the minimum 'overhang' behind the wheels. The same ideas have since appeared in many other projects – Bertone's own follow-ups, the Lancia Stratos (the name of which was later applied to a more workmanlike prototype rally car) and the Lamborghini Countach; and the later work of the stylist Giugiaro, who left Bertone to set up the Ital-Design group.

You could call the theme of the

A Grand Touring car? Or a saloon? The Citroen SM is a little of both. Officially it is a four seater touring car, but it has GT type lines and the sort of technical sophistication that makes it an enthusiast's car, including speed sensitive power steering, multiple hydraulic systems and a V6 Maserati engine

Top: Pininfarina's experimental Alfa Romeo 33 Spider of 1971 illustrates how the traditional open sports car can be incorporated within the modern wedge shape. It includes a roll-over protection bar. The same designer's Ferrari 512 wedge (above), built in 1970, is more startling if less realistic, with rear and three-quarter visibility a major problem

Below: The US government's scheme for Experimental Safety Vehicles prompted the Japanese Toyota company to build this two-seater sports car incorporating many of the ESV safety features. It is designed to protect the occupants in a head-on crash at 50mph and in a roll-over. The body is made of reinforced glass fibre. An electronic skid control system is fitted

Carabo a wedge-shape and that sums up the style for the advanced sporting car of the 1970s. It is adaptable for all sorts of sports car configurations. Giugiaro used it to extremes with a design using the front-wheel-drive Alfasud power unit, while Pininfarina have followed it with a couple of extraordinary Ferrari 512s, and much more practical open cars like the Alfa 33 Spider and the front-engined Alfetta Spider, both of which managed to incorporate a roll-over bar into the design without it looking distasteful. Such an arrangement allows a simple detachable roof panel and is probably the only way that future open cars will meet expected safety laws. The wedge shape has aerodynamic advantages. Properly used, it can eliminate the need for most of the aerofoil fins and wings which competition cars need to retain stability at very high speeds. Such things were in vogue amongst the stylists not long ago and some production cars have them, albeit more often as a racy gimmick than for practical purpose. But every wedge has its thin end and there are some problems attendant to this style. To look beautiful the front of the car must be low, which usually means too low for lighting regulations, so that headlamps have to be fitted under 'pop-up' retractable panels, and a pointed nose often leaves so little room that there is not even space for a proper spare wheel, let alone luggage in the front compartment—a problem, if the back is occupied by engine!

The big manufacturers are more reluctant to build 'show specials' than they used to be, but occasionally some give glimpses of their thoughts for the future and these are usually serious engineering projects rather than stylists' flights of fancy. Such a car is the Mercedes-Benz C111, built as a test bed for the German firm's experimental Wankel rotary engines. Distinctive if not particularly attractive, the C111 was no mere Motor Show mock-up. Several prototypes have been built and thoroughly tested—top performance is in the 160mph bracket. Mercedes' direct opponents in the saloon car market, BMW, showed

Above: Spectacular prototype built by BMW is the Turbo. Unlike some 'show cars' it has undergone serious running tests

Right: Bold Mercedes technical experiment is the C111—a racing-type coupé built to test their three and four rotor Wankel engines

the one-off Turbo in 1972 and a very practical prototype it was too, with a transverse mid-located 2 litre engine using a turbocharger, flexible plastic 'crush zones' front and rear, wide gull-wing doors and a well thought-out cockpit. General Motors have teased from time to time with mid-engined developments of the Corvette, while in Japan Nissan (Datsun) and Toyota have made serious attempts to integrate the features of an American government's 'safety car' into a sports coupé framework.

None of these manufacturers' 'idea cars' can be bought, however much money you have. The work of the small Italian specialists can be bought—and like the Dior dress, allows the rich to have today the style that the man in the street will be offered tomorrow. Even if 'tomorrow' is several years away.

A Question of Breeding

Ever since cars were first given closed tops there have been 'sports saloons', ones which went quicker, looked more rakish than the run-of-the-production line model. The science (or is it an art?) of tuning, of extracting latent potential from an engine, has its origins back in the roots of automobile history.

With the move towards economy family cars after the Second World War the gap between the ordinary touring car and the sports model enlarged. There were some exceptions of course, like most Jaguars, which did, and still do, combine many of the attributes of touring and sports

cars in their saloons, and the medium-capacity cars from the Italian firms of Alfa Romeo and Lancia, which have always had that certain sporting 'feel'. We have seen in an earlier chapter how the close-coupled 'two plus two' type of Grand Touring car developed out of the sports car mould. During the 1960s another breed grew up, also carrying name tags like 'GT' and 'S' – for Sport. They were the products of the large-scale manufacturers, cars which started off as unashamedly ordinary saloons dressed up to give them a sporting 'image'. Sometimes they were very much faster

and better handling than the basic product, sometimes they merely looked that bit more exciting.

It was the Mini that really started it all. Alec Issigonis' brilliant design – the basic 'tin box' with a wheel at each corner, and a disproportionate amount of interior space thanks to its transverse engine and gearbox unit – quickly became the major subject for the many small tuning firms around Britain. Its willing little

Mini-Coopers were very prominent in most branches of motor sport in the 1960s. Here John Rhodes and John Handley show their familiar rubber-burning cornering technique at Brands Hatch in the green and white Cooper works cars

The Mini built up a formidable record in international rallies, as well as making up a large proportion of national rally fields in their heyday. Above: Timo Makinen and Paul Easter on their way to victory in the 1966 Monte Carlo Rally

engine was based on a familiar design, and it was not too difficult to achieve a significant improvement over its modest 37 bhp output. A unique type of independent suspension made the Mini handle and go round corners much better than the average small car of the time. Whilst there was some reluctance at first to accept the Mini as a practical form of family transport, it did manage to cut across car snobbishness; young people bought them as handy runabouts and it became the smart thing for the rich to have as a 'fun' car.

In 1961, two years after the Mini's introduction, came the Mini-Cooper. The Cooper Car Company were at that time enjoying success with Formula Junior racing cars powered by basically the same BMC 'A' series engine. Their engines were tuned to perfection by a rather aristocratic boffin called Daniel Richmond, operating from a small works in a sleepy village called Downton in Hampshire. Between

them, John Cooper and Daniel Richmond proposed the idea of a special version of the Mini using a larger, twin-carburettor engine, front disc brakes and better instruments. BMC (now British Leyland) accepted the idea and the Mini-Cooper became a catalogued model, a 'hotted up' car which looked like the standard product, but went very much faster – and still enjoyed a manufacturer's guarantee!

Not only was the Mini-Cooper to be a commercial success but it was just what BMC's competition department needed. In the following years it won rallies and races all over the world and became Britain's most popular club competition car. The pressure of competition gave rise to the 'S' version with a proper racing engine – 1071 cc and 70 bhp, compared to 850 cc of the standard Mini and 997 cc and 55 bhp of the basic Cooper. That in turn led to two further versions, the 970 cc 'S' for the under 1000 racing category and the famous '1275' which was to bring three Monte Carlo Rally wins in a row (one was disallowed after a protest) and regularly defeat cars of much greater size and power in saloon car racing.

Joining up with the racers

The link between BMC and Cooper was prophetic in more than it gave the tuned car 'respectability'. It was the first of a whole series of British models which sought to achieve a go-faster image by associating with a successful racing team (in fact Gordini in France had linked with Renault many years before, and this association continues to this day). In due course, there were to be Brabham-Vauxhall Vivas and Holbay-engined Sunbeams, but it was Lotus–Cooper's arch-rivals on the track–who were next on the scene with the 1963 Lotus-Cortina.

Colin Chapman's modifications to Ford's newly announced conventional medium-sized saloon were far more comprehensive than those that created the Mini-Cooper. His Cortina used the Lotus twin-cam cylinder head which had been designed for racing and the Lotus Elan sports car. That gave it 105 bhp, an increase of more than 100 per cent over the standard Cortina. Unlike the Mini, the Cortina did not have enormous reserves of roadholding, so wider wheels were fitted, the suspension was lowered, the springs changed, a front anti-roll bar and rear axle

location 'A' bracket fitted. Furthermore, in an attempt to keep the weight down, the Lotus-Cortina had light-alloy doors, engine cover and trunk lid. The result was a startling car which at the time could see off virtually all of the sports cars of similar size and price.

The Lotus-Cortina's introduction coincided with Ford's increasing interest in performance as a factor in car sales. They had intro-

duced a so-called GT version of the first Capri, itself a notably unattractive fastback version of the heavily stylized Consul Classic. That Capri was not a great success, but the GT label did crop up again for a version of the Cortina. This was more like the Mini-Cooper in concept than the Lotus, being a more powerful and differently trimmed version of the standard car at a relatively small additional price. Between them, the

Top: One of the highlights of touring car racing in the mid-1960s was the exuberant driving of Jim Clark in a works Lotus-Cortina, here at Brands Hatch in 1964

Above: Hill and Wood negotiating a Welsh hairpin in one of the many Escorts in British national rallies

Cortina GT and Lotus-Cortina enjoyed a highly successful competition career. As time went on the Lotus variant became a little tamer (the fragile lightweight panels were soon abandoned) and eventually lost the Lotus name tag altogether, while the GT variant became a big seller and had a widespread influence on Ford's future product policy. It is no exaggeration to say that these cars have brought a great improvement to Ford's standard product in terms of performance, handling and controls.

The Ford Escort which won the London-Mexico World Cup Rally in 1970 (below) was a hybrid using an Escort Twin Cam bodyshell and an 1800cc pushrod engine. As a result of its success, Ford put an Escort variant called the Mexico into production, using the 1600cc Cortina GT engine, and initiated races (bottom) especially for them

When the Ford Escort came along, as a smaller, cheaper car than the Cortina, the performance emphasis was transferred to that. There was a 1300GT Escort from the start but the really exciting variant was the Lotus Twin-Cam engined version. It was designed from the outset as a competition car and on the road it was a revelation, with the combination of tremendous performance and quick response of a type that most medium-priced 'traditional' sports cars could not begin to match. Almost from the time it was announced in Spring,

1968, the Escort Twin Cam was a winner and it was to form the highly successful mainstay of Ford's European racing and rally programme for three years.

Ford's huge involvement in all aspects of motor sport had included financing the development of formula 1 and formula 2 racing engines built by Cosworth Engineering. The formula 2 engine, known as the FVA, utilised the Ford Cortina cylinder block. When the time came to look for a replacement for the trusty Lotus Twin-Cam, Ford needed to look no further than the FVA, which had two camshafts operating four valves per cylinder (two inlet, two exhaust). A simplified version called the BDA was built and the Escort so equipped with 120bhp became the RS1600, which quickly took the place of the Escort Twin Cam as the ideal privateers' rally car. Like the black Model T 30 years before, Escort Twin Cams and RS1600s could be any colour that the customer wanted providing it was white, and in the weekly magazine reports of British national and club rallies it was rare to find a photograph of anything other than a white Escort with a fashionable black bonnet!

Rallying did a great deal to encourage and develop these high performance models from the big manufacturers. Among Ford's successes

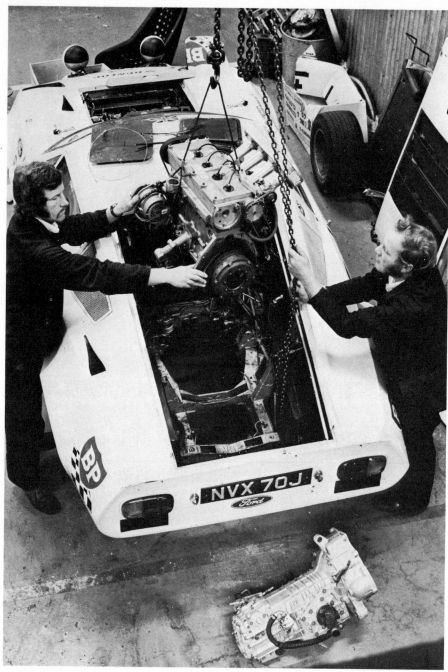

was victory in the gruelling World Cup Rally from London to Mexico in 1970. For this event they had built some special Escorts starting with the strengthened Twin Cam/RS1600 bodyshell but using an enlarged version of the 1600cc pushrod Cortina engine, which they considered might be less temperamental with the difficult conditions and sub-standard fuel along the Rally's incredible 16 000 mile route. The idea eventually gave rise to the production Escort Mexico, built by Ford's Advanced Vehicle Operation and using the same Escort RS1600 shell with the Cortina GT 1600cc engine. It is perhaps the epitome of today's 'sports saloon cars' – an

equivalent of the pre-war MG. It goes and handles well, looks a bit racy, can acquit itself without disgrace in competition in near-standard form, and is relatively cheap to buy and run.

Ride your personal pony

Ford must also take the credit for starting a parallel wave of 'performance-image' cars in America. In 1962 they exhibited a nice little mid-engined two-seater called the Mustang. It was not developed, but another styling exercise of the same era, called the Mach 2, was adopted for production, and given the Mustang name. It was Ford Dearborn's bid in the youth market – a

Above, left: In 1970 the Escort Twin Cam became the Escort RS1600, as the Ford-Cosworth BDA engine was substituted for the older Lotus Twin Cam unit. The BDA found widespread application for other types of competition cars including sports/racing and formula 2 cars. Ford's own rally prototype, the GT70, started life with a German V6 engine but was eventually fitted with a BDA

Above: A feature of US TransAm touring car races is mandatory pit stops for fuel and/or tyres. Here fuel spills after a hurried refuelling stop for Jim Hall's Chevrolet Camaro Z28

Right: Two of the 'performance' breed of US pony cars that have competed with distinction in TransAm racing – Pontiac Firebird and Chevrolet Camaro, both of which are offered in 'competition' versions

conventional, front-engined, live rear axle American car using existing components, and around the

size of the industry's 'compacts' of the time. Its important difference was the styling, which was a sporty blend of traditional American and GT coupé-type lines. It was not a sports car, neither was it an ordinary saloon. Ford called it a 'personal' car.

The Mustang was a fantastic commercial success. Within five months of its introduction in April 1964 it was third best-selling model on the US market. It was not long before a multiplicity of performance options became available for it, including V8 engines, wider wheels and tyres. Mustangs were raced on both sides of the Atlantic, and as anyone who saw the award-winning film *Un*

homme et une femme will know, Ford entered them in European rallies. Carroll Shelby produced a special version which Ford offered as a catalogue model called the GT350. It had the AC Cobra's tuned V8 engine and a number of changes to brakes and suspension. In the meantime the Cobra name had been applied to the big 7-litre V8 engine which was offered in 'muscle car' versions of full-size and 'intermediate' American models, tied in with the NASCAR oval-track stock-car racing programme.

As the Mustang grew more powerful it also gained bulk—and weight—until in 1970 and 1971 the wider engine options were dropped from

the range because of the difficulties of meeting anti-pollution laws and the ever-increasing cost of insurance. Connoisseurs of the *marque* still look to the early GT350s—one of which ran at 150mph for 12 hours at Daytona in 1968—as the best of the bunch.

Naturally the Mustang's success brought competitors from the other car makers, giving rise to a whole new breed of so-called 'pony cars'. Chevrolet came up with the Camaro, Pontiac with the similar Firebird, American Motors with the Javelin, while the Dodge Challenger. and Plymouth Barracuda formed Chrysler's bid in a battle which took place not only in the dealer

successful mixture of saloon and GT characteristics. It also followed American practice in offering a tremendous range of specification options including four different engine sizes, plus a couple more in German versions sold in Europe and subsequently as part of the Lincoln-Mercury line in the US. As the Mustang had in America, the Capris created a new sort of saloon car—a practical four seater that looked like a less compromising GT car. It was soon imitated all over the world—in the Opel Manta from Germany, the Japanese Toyota Celica, and the Renault 15 and 17s for example. (Fiat's coupé sport variant of the 124 saloon, in fact preceded the Capri in its announcement.)

Left: Rolling start of a TransAm race in the days (1970) when all of Detroit's manufacturers were officially or semi-officially represented. The Mustangs of George Follmer and Parnelli Jones lead Ed Leslie's Camaro Swede Savage's Plymouth

Below: A turbocharged BMW 2002 leads a Porsche 911 at Brands Hatch in 1969, and (bottom) a BMW 3·0 CS at Spa in 1972

Meanwhile, Ford had charged their German company with producing a competition version of the Capri. Following the lines of the Escort Twin Cam, this used a powerful version of the V6 engine produced by the Weslake Company in England in a special model for sale known as the RS2600. This was the spearhead of the Ford racing team in the European Touring Car Championship.

We have already seen that those who govern motor sport have problems deciding what to allow in competition under the guise of 'sports car'. The definition of a saloon or a touring car can present similar difficulties. Of the cars contesting international touring car races in the late 1960s, the Fords (Cortinas and Escorts) and the BMWs (2002s) were unquestionably saloon cars, but they were competing against Porsche 911s and Alfa Romeo GT coupés. This was so because, providing sufficient numbers had been built, the classification depended on the car's interior dimensions. Those

showrooms but in TransAm road racing on circuits all over the USA. As with the Cortina in Europe, this programme did a great deal to improve the standard car and the range of equipment available for it, so that it became possible by judicious selection from the vast options lists to buy a car from the factory which could measure up pretty well in terms of handling and roadholding with the better European products.

The 'pony car' crossed the Atlantic in 1969. Ford of Britain had long been rumoured to have a sports car on the stocks and when the new Capri appeared it turned out not to be a sports car as such, rather a

minimum dimensions were altered – which excluded the Porsche but left in the Alfas.

By 1972 the saloon car racing contest had developed into a battle between the factory-entered Capri RS2600s, taking full advantage of the very free modifications the rules allowed, and BMW's 3·0 CS coupé.

Both meet the saloon car rules. Both are reasonable four-seaters, yet most people would nominate the Capri as a saloon and the elegant and expensive BMW, a modern Grand Touring car. It has never been easy to decide what is and what isn't a sports car, but it has never been more difficult than it is today.

Above: Powerful modern sporting saloons are quite able to hold their own with 'proper' sports and GT cars. These Ford Capri RS2600s are racing in the 1972 Tourist Trophy saloon car race at Silverstone, but during that year they also performed with distinction in classic long-distance sports car races at Le Mans and the Nürburgring, where they were placed 10th, 11th, 6th and 7th respectively. In the 1973 four-hour race at Monza, the lap speeds of lightweight 3-litre Capris and BMWs exceeded 130mph

Index

Acknowledgments The publishers are grateful to the following individuals and organizations for the illustrations in this book: Aston Martin Lagonda Ltd; *Autocar;* Hugh Bishop; BMW; British Leyland Motor Corporation; Michael Bowler; Detroit Public Library; Fiat; Ford Motor Co Ltd; Geoffrey Goddard; Gulf Oil Co; David Hodges; Ray Hutton; Jaguar Cars Ltd; Louis Klemantaski; Lamborghini; Lancia; Charles A. Lytle; Morgan Motor Co Ltd; *Motor;* National Motor Museum; René Pari; Pininfarina; Porsche; RaceReporters; Rolls-Royce Motors Ltd; Nigel Snowdon; David Stone; Toyota; Vauxhall Motors Ltd; Andrew Whyte.